Super Commuter Couples

Super Commuter Couples

Staying Together When a Job Keeps You Apart

Megan Bearce, LMFT

Lora,

Thank you!

Equanimity Press
Minneapolis

Most names and identifying details of the individuals in this book have been changed to protect their privacy. The author and publisher of this book intend for this publication to provide accurate information. It is sold with the understanding that it is meant to complement, not substitute for, professional medical and/or psychological services.

While the author has made every effort to provide accurate Internet addresses and contact information at the time of publication, neither the publisher nor the author assume any responsibility for error, or for changes that occur after publication. Further, the publisher nor the author do not have any control over and do not assume any responsibility for third-party websites or their content.

978-0-9899457-1-4

Printed in the United States of America.

Cover design by Dean Carpentier
Cover photo ©2010 Dean Carpentier
Author photograph ©2012 Joseph Forman
Interior design by Dorie McClelland, springbookdesign.com

For information:
Equanimity Press
www.equanimitypress.net
700 Twelve Oaks Center Dr., Suite 226,
Wayzata, MN 55391

To my village

Contents

Introduction

One day, in retrospect, the years of struggle
will strike you as the most beautiful.
—Sigmund Freud

I n addition to being a licensed therapist, I am the wife of a super commuter. If you had told me a few years ago what our life would look like today—with my husband Ian leaving for a "dream job" in New York early on Monday morning each week and returning home to Minneapolis Friday evening, I would have laughed and said, "No way!" Having barely escaped our personal financial meltdown that started in May 2009 when we were living in Los Angeles—triggered by the perfect storm of the real estate crash, the stock market crash, and the birth of our second child—I thought we were all settled in to re-build our lives in Minneapolis. Little did I know that once again our world was about to be turned upside down.

During the decision-making process of whether or not to launch into a super commuting relationship, we had to make tough decisions and we had to rationalize. Unlike other business disciplines, my husband's work on the production side of advertising does not offer an advanced degree. In this business there is only one way to prove oneself and that is by demonstrating unique skills and resources. That being the cold reality, we had to weigh the amount of exposure and experience he would gain by working at one of the premier special effects companies in the world against the difficulty of separation. We told ourselves and we told other people that by going to New York to live and work, Ian would be paid to receive the equivalent of an MBA degree in his industry. Other considerations important to him were the quality and integrity of the employees, the work environment and corporate culture, and the fact that many employees at the company highly value family life.

Add into the mix the instability of his current job in Minneapolis, plus the security of a big job with a big company, and a super commuting arrangement began to sound more and more appealing. And finally, even if manna rained from the heavens and we magically found a way to move east, what if Ian didn't like the job—or worse, what if he got laid off? It was 2010 and the economy and housing market were still limping along with no prospects of a meaningful turnaround.

After carefully considering the pros and cons, the pros won out and we decided to take a giant leap of faith into the unknown and we are now well past our two-year anniversary. And the fact is, we are hardly alone. Today there are literally millions of people who are doing the same thing we are doing in one form or another.

For this book I interviewed two-dozen people from Costa Rica, South Africa, and across the United States who were involved in a super commuter relationship (names and other identifying information have been changed to protect privacy). The lessons they have to impart are as diverse as they are helpful to those contemplating a plunge into such a relationship.

These lessons are enough to fill a book. Many of them are included in this one. May you find insights and encouragement from what my husband and I continue to experience and from what I have gleaned from others in the United States and beyond who share this ever more popular lifestyle.

If so, then this book has fulfilled its purpose.

Meet the Super Commuters

1

The Super Commuting Phenomenon

What do we leave behind when we cross each frontier?
Each moment seems split in two: melancholy for what
was left behind and the excitement of entering a new land.
—*Ernesto Guevara*

My motivation for writing this book has as much to do with our children as it does with my husband and me. Our daughter Katherine was three and a half years old and our son Austin almost two when Ian started his job in New York. Given where they were developmentally, they each handled it differently. Our son seemed less impacted initially, but as he has grown older, he has become more vocal about missing his father and asking when he will be home. Katherine has always been close to her father and as an emotionally intense child; her reaction to him leaving her every week was often traumatic. Sunday evenings and Monday mornings were usually and sometimes still are especially difficult since over the weekend we had crammed in as much quality "dad time" as possible— and yet, at the same time, doing as many household projects as we could along with the myriad of other tasks, paperwork, and scheduling that Ian and I rarely have time to discuss in detail during the week. It was heart-wrenching for me (and for Ian and me, on Sunday evenings) to watch Katherine lying in her bed sobbing, missing her daddy even before he left and pleading with him to stop going to New York. I could only commiserate with her and explain that we all missed him.

I would also remind her of the fun things we had done that weekend or would be doing again in just a few short days.

Sometimes that calmed her. Usually it didn't. And I would have to confess to her that I truly didn't know when he would be able to stop making these long weekly trips a half a continent away. I was walking that fine line that parents walk when they don't want to burden their child with their own emotions while at the same encouraging the child to express her feelings honestly. If she felt sad, which she often did, it was best for her to express that sadness.

Such is one tiny facet of the daily life of a "super commuting" family.

So what exactly is a super commuter? However one defines the term, essentially it refers to a new category of employee who lives in one city and commutes a great distance to his or her job in another city, via any mode of transportation. Due to the sometimes vast distances involved, it is often more economical and work-efficient to not return home on a daily basis, but rather on weekends only. This phenomenon is by no means limited to the United States. The *Financial Times* of London ran an article in December of 2011 in which it highlighted the growing trend of super commuting in Europe, profiling employees who do weekly commutes between London and such Continental cities as Amsterdam and Prague.

When I initially started researching the topic of super commuters I was shocked by what I discovered. The Rudin Center for Transportation Policy and Management at New York University has become the preeminent source on the international phenomenon of super commuting. Led by its director, Mitchell Moss, the Center published a study in February of 2012 entitled "The Emergence of the 'Super-Commuter'" that cited trends and data on super commuting based on U.S. census data from 2009. According to their research, which looked at the ten largest labor workforces (or "sheds") in the United States, the Rudin Center estimated that the number of super commuters in those locations ranged anywhere from 3 percent to 13 percent of the workforce, depending on the county. That may seem like a manageable number, but when you multiply even 3 percent by 114 million people—the approximate number of full-time workers in the United States in 2012—you compute a total number of 3.42 million super commuters. This total is only an estimation of course, but no matter how you do the math from whatever source, the fact remains that that Ian and I are in fairly crowded company!

The Center's study has generated a wealth of statistics and the numbers are enlightening. It found, for example, that Los Angeles County alone had 233,000 super commuters in 2009, an increase of 76.7 percent from the number in 2002, with the largest groups commuting to Los Angeles from San Diego (78,300 people) and San Francisco (35,700 people). And although it is 100 miles between Tucson and Phoenix—the Sun Corridor, as it's called—more than 54,000 people have chosen to make that commute. As a percentage of the workforce, the counties with the largest number of super commuters were Harris, Texas (where Houston is located: 261,000) and Dallas (176,000) and these figures represented 13.2 percent of each county's workforce. In addition to the routes of Dallas-Fort Worth to Houston and San Antonio to Houston, which grew 218 percent and 116 percent respectively, rounding out the top five most popular "twin cities" for super commuters are Boston to Manhattan, which more than doubled between 2002 and 2009; Yakima to Seattle; and San Jose to Los Angeles. The county in which Ian and I live in Minnesota (Hennepin County, which includes the metro area of Minneapolis but not St. Paul) had 40,000 super commuters in 2009, equaling 5.2 percent of the workforce of the county.

Included in the Rudin Center study are findings that peg the average age of a super commuter at 29. However, an increasing number of older workers, including baby boomers, are joining this trend with several major cities showing workers aged 55 and over comprising an ever larger segment of the super commuting community. Interestingly, the Center's findings also indicated that the average income of super commuters approximates $40,000 per year, leading them to state in their report that while some super commuters are top executives flying to work, more and more are middle-class earners who might choose to live in less expensive areas and drive or take public transportation to their job.

In other words, the Center's study suggests that many people who commute long distances to work are forced to do so for economic reasons, the three most salient I summarize as (1) the crash of the housing market, (2) high unemployment rates, especially for "higher end" positions, and (3) a shifting workplace environment in which an increasing number of employees are engaged in nontraditional work habits such as telecommuting and working from home. If, for example, an individual loses his job and then finds another job in a distant city that addresses his family's financial needs—or financial crisis, as the case may be—that's all well and good. But what if that individual can't sell his home and move because the mortgage is under water? To take another example, what if the city where the new job is located has a substantially higher cost of living compared to where his current home is located? What choices do he or she and his family have? What are they to do?

The oil fields in Alaska and the hydraulic fracturing in the Midwest are two examples of Wild West-like gold rushes that people are choosing to pursue. Williston, North Dakota, is the epicenter of what is commonly referred to as fracking, the process of injecting fluid at high pressures deep into the ground to fracture shale rock and release the natural gas or oil inside. A *Chicago Tribune* article dubbed it "the biggest oil boom in the lower 48 states." It went on to report that this town had a population of 17,000 in 2010, but due to extremely high-paying jobs across skills sets, the town is now the "fastest growing micropolitan area" in the United States, with its population topping 40,000 in early 2013. The resulting housing shortage has triggered sky-high rents, and so many employers have built temporary camps for their employees to live in while their families stay back home, hundreds and thousands of miles away.

Kelly and her husband Aaron, who you will hear more from later, had a small electrical company in northern Minnesota that was struggling to survive. They decided that the best choice for them—perhaps their *only* choice—was for Aaron to super commute to Alaska for four-week stints to work as an electrician on an oil pipeline. This sort of decision to split the family for the sake of financial security certainly seemed to offer the only sensible choice for Ian and me as well.

The complexities and intricacies of super commuting fascinate me not only personally, but also professionally. As a licensed marriage and family therapist I am curious about relationship dynamics and why people do what they do and how they navigate challenges, create new opportunities for themselves, and foster resilience. As the partner of a super commuter, I have the personal experience of being in what to many people still seems like a non-traditional relationship. I am a single mom during the week (what I refer to in this book as a "weekday widow") and I can share firsthand what has worked, what hasn't, and the ups and downs that go hand in hand with this emotional rollercoaster ride of super commuting.

I eventually got to the point where I could "not not" write this book. For better or for worse, super commuting had become a part of my life and the lives of those I love most in this world. Writing this book has been therapeutic for me as I look back and process our often convoluted journey from Los Angeles to Minneapolis to New York. The experience has not all been bad—not by any means—but having my core family split apart for five out of seven days every week of every month of the year is challenging, at best. I very much hope that what Ian and I have learned on this journey we have taken together can serve as a valuable resource for couples either currently involved or soon to be involved in a super commuting relationship, as well as for therapists who might have a client who is either a super commuter or the spouse of one. But this book is not intended just for commuting couples. What has arisen from my own experiences and from the experiences of others like me are tips and lessons and themes that I think *all* couples can utilize to help strengthen their own relationships.

As may be obvious to you by now, to me as a licensed therapist, the statistics cited above by the Rubin Center—while interesting and startling—are more than just a jumble of facts and figures. They speak directly to the heart of what underlies a modern phenomenon that in former days would have seemed unthinkable. Can anyone honestly imagine Cliff Huxtable in *The Cosby Show* informing his wife Clair that starting Monday he is going to commute from Brooklyn to a medical facility in Chicago every week? No, of course not, but that's because that show is set in the 1980s, a galaxy away from the demands, pitfalls, and realities of our modern twenty-first century society. As the statistics confirm, many of today's super commuters are Dr. Huxtable's age (i.e., baby boomers) in the television series, and that trend, too, is on the rise.

A search of the Internet for information on super commuting reveals articles that focus primarily on the commuter, typically male, and the logistics of his weekly or monthly commute. Harder to find are articles in support of those left behind. Many of the women and men I have spoken with who lived at home while their partner super commuted claimed that the hardest part of the separation was not having the daily support of their partner. While many couples in a more traditional work environment may have one or both partners working long and demanding hours, they at least have the comfort of a goodnight kiss or the quick face to face chat in the morning to check in about the day ahead. Such intimacies mean everything and lie at the core of most successful relationships. Then add in the challenges of raising children and not having that partner helping with morning breakfast or bedtime routines or daycare pick-up or teacher meetings or any number of other "normal" weekday activities, and their super commute can seem almost like the untimely death of that spouse.

But since that person is alive, the weekday widow (or widower) has not the same freedom to grieve the loss, a condition more accurately referred to as "ambiguous loss." I introduce the term at this time simply to emphasize that "ambiguous loss" and "super commuting" are concepts that inexorably go hand in hand. Ambiguous loss, which I will expand on in subsequent chapters, is a term that is becoming more widely recognized and appreciated due to the work of Dr. Pauline Boss, a leader in the field. Her book *Loss, Trauma, and Resilience* (W.W. Norton, New York, 2006) analyzes how ambiguous loss differs from regular loss in that the person at issue may return home but not necessarily in the same emotional state as when he or she left. A super commuter interviewed by American Public Media's *Marketplace* started out with this promise to his wife: "We'll try it for a year and see how it goes." Seven years later the couple is still married, but the super commuter sees no reason to end his routine and return to a more traditional lifestyle. If he did decide to end it, he would be facing another sort of challenge. The "re-entry period," which I will also expand on in a later chapter, can highlight the feelings of ambiguous loss on a weekly basis. Daily life from Monday through Friday goes on without the commuter and how does that dynamic change the family and the commuter? How do they fit back into the family life when they come home for the weekend? And what are the consequences when the super commute ends due to retirement or job change or transfer? Will the relationships be changed for better or for worse? These and related questions will be addressed in this book.

People come to this crossroad of deciding whether to super commute for various reasons. Three of the most obvious are steeped in financial opportunity or necessity: a new and better job, the loss of a job, or a company downsizing that forces an employee to leave the company or relocate whether he or she likes it or not.

Another reason for super commuting is that it simply comes with the job. Consider, for example, the military. If you are a member of the armed forces, you usually don't have the luxury of living and working close to home throughout your term of service. If you don't want to move to where the Army or Navy wants to move you, you can either retire if circumstances warrant or go AWOL—the latter course of action not being recommended. Even as I type this, the Winter 2012 issue of *USAA Magazine*, published by USAA, a company offering financial services for military families, ran an article about the difficulty military spouses face finding employment in a new location or getting re-licensed when the service member is required to relocate. Such difficulties can lead to the spouse staying put and not going with his or her partner, as was the case of one couple profiled in the article. A military super commuter couple made do with one partner living in Alaska and the other choosing to stay behind in Arkansas due to the cost and time to obtain a teaching license in Alaska. In my own situation, my need to be re-licensed somewhere close to New York City played into our decision not to move the family to New York. It was not the only factor, nor was it the most important factor, but it certainly had a role in the decision-making process.

I have thus structured this book to address a broad range of topics—the good, the bad, and the practical—related to super commuting. Most chapters and topics are reinforced by interviews with present-day super commuters or their partners who have shared with me the costs and benefits of their experiences. These interviews include three with military personnel, since as we have discussed, members of the armed forces are ipso facto part of the trend. (In fact, it can be argued that members of any country's armed forces were the world's original super commuters!) There are also stories of couples with young kids and with no kids, couples who are married, and couples who never intend to marry, gay couples and straight couples. Certain of these couples have been living a super commute lifestyle for more than twenty years, while others are just starting out commuting between small towns and big cities, or between the United States and Costa Rica, for example. Following their stories are chapters in which I combine my professional expertise as a licensed marriage and family therapist with my personal experience as the partner of a super commuter along with all that I have learned in talking with the participants. Here I analyze the core issues of what a couple should contemplate carefully if they are considering a super commute or even if they are already doing it. In this analysis I have also peppered the text with practical suggestions and tips for saving money, navigating travel, and keeping your sanity—among other things. In addition, I have included related questions for the reader to reflect upon for themselves and their relationship. As the saying goes, "life is a journey" and at times it can be very stressful. But sometimes living life "out of the box" can become a preferred way of living that allows spouses and their children to grow in ways that until now they might not have imagined or predicted.

Even if your typical Monday morning commute does not require you to navigate an airport security checkpoint to catch a flight to your full-time job or involve saying goodbye to your family for the next five days, I believe you will enjoy a glimpse into the journey that others are taking and thus find value and insight into your own relationship.

2

A Super Commuter Pioneer

Life is what you make it. Always has been, always will be.
—Eleanor Roosevelt

In August of 1995, after nearly ten years of married life in Washington D.C., Liz and her husband David decided to move to Minnesota where Liz's family was living. They had wanted to move for a while and after some discussion of the subject, David approached his boss at the non-profit organization he worked for and asked him about the possibility of opening a satellite office in Minneapolis. After conferring with other senior executives, his boss agreed to the proposal. And so began David's super commute between the two cities and wherever else his services were required. On a typical week he left home on Thursday and returned on Sunday.

Liz and David's story is an insightful one since it involves nearly seventeen years of childrearing. They now have three children and the two oldest ones were three and one when the family relocated to Minnesota. For them, having their father away so much especially over the weekends is simply the way life is.

"It's dad's work," they often rationalize according to Liz. "It's no big deal."

It was a bigger deal for their mother, but having her parents and siblings close by made the transition much smoother, as did finding playgroups, a night out with girlfriends, and getting together with other families for Friday night Shabbat dinners. As many women experience, she didn't always know what kind of help she needed, but she knew she needed to have several sources of support waiting in the wings for when the need arose. She therefore made it a point to cultivate connections. She compares the times when her husband is out of town, especially when the kids were little, to "a marathon I could handle until that last grueling mile. The closer the hour came for him to return home—for me to cross the finish line—the more agitated and exhausted I became, and the less patient. Unfortunately this less than positive attitude was often what greeted David when he arrived home rather than the appreciation and respect I felt for his hard work during most of the week." The re-entry period—both short-term and long-term—is a tough one for many of the people I spoke with, perhaps for an obvious reason. At the core of re-entry is the joy of being back together coupled with the sadness and dread of having to say goodbye again in the not-too-distant future. Arguing between couples can become quite common at times like these because arguing is a form of self-protection; it's easier to be mad than sad; so being upset with your spouse during these sensitive hours becomes an all too frequent and damaging occurrence.

Sometimes the coming together is filled with emotions and information that has accumulated during the weekly separation, as well as with simple fatigue. Susan Pease Gadoua, LCSW, wrote a *Psychology Today* article titled: "To Connect, Women Want to Talk and Men Want Sex—How Do Straight Couples Reconcile?" In the article Ms. Gadoua discusses the differences that occur when heterosexual couples try to resolve stress in their relationship. According to her, "When women are stressed out, talking literally soothes them because the calming (and bonding) hormone called oxytocin is released in the female brain. When men are stressed, testosterone is released and getting physical is an obvious outlet."

This observation summons to mind a solution that David related to me in regards to whenever he arrived home to a frazzled wife.

If Liz was upset about a situation, he learned to listen to his wife first and try to offer solutions later. That simple rule of thumb often allowed her to lower her stress level sufficiently by "talking through" a problem on her own with David doing nothing but listening. It is also similar to a tool that Ian and I have worked out for when we talk on the phone during the week. We first determine the mood and sensitivities of the other before launching in to a deeper conversation or problem-solving discussion.

"Humor," was Liz's immediate reply when I asked her how she copes with life's many challenges. "It's vital to maintain a sense of humor, even when the kids are out of control, you have no help, and you feel as though the walls are caving in on you. A little laughter can go a long way at times like these. Even better is when you have other moms who can laugh along with you without casting judgment."

She then proceeded to tell me about an incident that happened when her son was young. She had been spending the better part of a day in the bathroom trying to toilet-train him when her husband suddenly announced that he was home. Their son wanted to impress his father with his newfound skill and proceeded to do so while *sitting down* on the toilet. Laughing, her husband said, "I'll take it from here Liz, thank you very much."

She said to me with a chuckle, "I did the best I could. I didn't think anything of not teaching him to stand up. And that's just one example of how we were each just doing the best we could in the moment. There were other male milestones that my husband missed out on, but they ended up becoming family stories that we laugh about together years later." On a more serious note, she was quick to emphasize that her husband is very engaged as both a father and a partner and she credits these attributes as key reasons why things continue to work out for them and why their marriage remains so strong.

Because Liz's husband David was willing to share his experiences of being a super commuter, I was able to learn more not only about their relationship but also the reality of what a super commute is actually like for the commuter and how he and his wife have managed to make it work so well for so long. When David initially approached his boss about moving from Washington D.C. and setting up a satellite office in Minneapolis, telecommuting of any kind was extremely rare. An online forum at PBS.com dated January 14, 1997, entitled "Telecommuting: Dream Come True?" stated that although telecommuting had its initial start in the 1980s as a way to reduce commuting-related pollution, it was not until the 1990s when fax machines, cell phones, and email began to gain traction that telecommuting came into its own. As a result of these innovations the workplace began to shift, and David credits his "great boss" with sensing what was coming and turning this experimental situation into a long-term work arrangement. During the mid-1990s the Internet was still in its infancy (as a frame of reference, America Online as it was called back then was just starting to mail out their sign-up computer discs) and David often had to write his own computer code script just to get online. He wanted to make it work and in an era where a typical management tenet was, "If I can't see an employee working, he probably isn't working," it was groundbreaking territory that his boss was opening up to David. In return for his boss's trust, David submitted a weekly report of what he was working on and what progress he was making with each item. Ultimately he felt that he expected more of himself than did his boss and they both agreed that there needed to be realistic boundaries placed around work. In sum, David's super commute worked well because of the trust and respect of both his wife *and* his boss!

Twenty years later as the company's associate managing director, David has a firm policy of not emailing staff on the weekends or late in the evening unless he absolutely must. Even then, he prefaces the message with, "I don't need you to respond to this tonight." When David's boss in Washington would take a vacation, he would tell his staff not to call him even if the building were on fire. That determination to separate one's professional life from his personal life is something David continues to insist upon to this day.

When I asked David about the pros and cons of his decision to super commute, he had several positive points to convey. He said in the beginning he was the only one in a company of 1,100 employees who either super commuted or telecommuted on a regular weekly basis. Five years later he helped to write his company's telecommuting policy defining what technology would be needed and which employees and which positions offered a good fit for this sort of arrangement. This report, combined with increasing traffic jams on every major road in the D.C. area, led to many employees telecommuting one day per week. Today, working out of his New Jersey office, David reports that 85 to 90 percent of his employees work "away" at least one day per week. For the past three years his office has been recognized as one of the best places to work in the state of New Jersey, and David maintains that having established this flex schedule option for qualified employees is a major factor in receiving that honor. He is convinced that his employees deeply appreciate his trust and flexibility, which in turn improves their morale and job performance, which in turn contributes to a healthy work environment.

When I asked David if he had gleaned any travel tips during his years of super commuting that he would like to pass along, he laughed and asked if I'd seen *Up in the Air*, a movie that offers a glimpse into the life of a man (played by George Clooney) whose job has him flying almost every day of the year. He said when he first started working he loved to travel but didn't pay too much attention to perks. Now he pays keen attention to them. In order to offset the downside of having to be away from home and family, he recommends staying in a comfortable hotel, enjoying a good meal, and above all, exercising on a daily basis to reduce stress and clear the mind. He compared this lifestyle to running a marathon (ironically the same comparison his wife used) in that one needs to take care of oneself and pace oneself or surely burnout will rear its ugly head. He was adamant that this lifestyle is not for everyone and it is important to know oneself as well as one's spouse before rushing in.

"Super commuting consumes a lot of hours and often involves a lot of hours alone," he added, "but I stay connected with others via a running group and my daily interactions with people on the phone." He also advises the partner who stays at home to find his or her own means of purpose and independence. "If a person's whole reason for being is intertwined with his partner's daily life, he will essentially lose a piece of himself each and every week."

As David said this I was reminded of a favorite passage of mine written by Kahlil Gibran in *The Prophet*: ". . . And stand together yet not too near together: For the pillars of the temple stand apart, And the oak tree and the Cyprus tree grow not in each other's shadows."

A closing thought which comprises words of advice more for companies than their employees: David didn't think his company could attract as many Gen X or Gen Y employees if it didn't offer flex work, which by now has become the norm in business rather than the exception. He then went on to reflect on the spectrum of management styles he has experienced during his career. When he started working, the senior management of most companies was comprised of what might best be called "traditionalists." In what was voted the fourth most influential management book of the 20th century, *The Human Side of Enterprise*, Douglas McGregor, a professor at MIT's Sloan School of Management and former president of Antioch College, presented his concepts of Theory X management (which assumes that employees dislike work, are inherently lazy, and will shirk whenever the opportunity arises) and Theory Y management (which assumes that workers can be highly motivated and want to do well if given the right incentives). Through his own example of work ethics David helped straddle the chasm between Theory X and Theory Y and again he credits his forward-thinking boss with much of his success in bridging that gap and enlightening the company's senior management. But after talking with him at length on the subject, I am convinced that his determination to make his career work well for himself and for his family played an equally important role in that success.

When I asked him specific questions about his family, David gave answers similar to those of his wife whom I interviewed on a separate occasion. He agreed that the biggest challenges of their super commuting relationship were during the early years when having three young children made daily life more difficult for his wife than for him. They both mentioned that one of the most important tools for them was meeting on a regular basis to review and arrange schedules as far out in advance as possible. Doing so, they believed, helped prevent surprises and aided in planning quality time together. Liz was working too, building her private practice and as such, they encountered many of the challenges dual career households face. Another perk of his telecommuting arrangement is that it allows him to be flexible when working from home and therefore to attend his children's activities during the week more than other fathers he knew. He also mentioned the myth out there that the person commuting has the better of it because he doesn't have to get up during the night or take care of the children's needs. But he said that when he is away, he typically works non-stop all-day and even into the night. Combining fatigue with the stress of traveling, he often walks in the door at home utterly exhausted, only to be greeted by a long list of home responsibilities that demand his attention.

"Super commuting does not allow workloads to be balanced out on a day-to-day basis," he commented somewhat plaintively. "They come in bunches for super commuters and for their spouses, and the result can sometimes be overwhelming."

Earlier, Liz made the comparison between super commuting and running a marathon. Books that teach you how to train for a marathon talk about things like motivation, goals, nutrition, support from running partners and recovery, all points that Liz and David seem to have done a good job incorporating into their lives and their relationship.

3

Resentment

Unexpressed emotions will never die.
They are buried alive and will come forth later in uglier ways.
—Sigmund Freud

Resentment. It is not a pretty word and it does not evoke pretty images. But many women, myself included, find it to be an all-too-pervasive emotion in a super commuting relationship.

For me, as is true for most weekday widows, resentment is most likely to rear its ugly head when I'm tired or when the kids are acting up or when stress levels are approaching the red zone. It can be quickly ignited by something as innocent as my husband telling me on the phone about an exciting event he had attended—a *New Yorker* sponsored art opening, for example, or a fancy dinner at a hot new restaurant—and the only sound I am hearing is the swoosh of blood in my ears. A tool I have developed for times like these is to take a deep breath and think of something I am grateful for that is the result of our super commuting relationship. (Often such thoughts focus on the quality time I am able to enjoy with my children or that I am able to have a part-time career I find fulfilling.) This usually helps to ease the "pity party" I'm throwing for myself and to shift my mood from anger to acceptance and sometimes even to gratitude. Ian and I also have developed the habit of asking each other at the outset of each telephone call how the other is doing. That way we can sense each other's mood and thus set the tone for the conversation.

One of the best examples of the how intense and complex resentment can be is from the book *Mommies Who Drink*. In it, the author and narrator, Brett Paesel, a former actress and now a stay-at-home mom of a toddler, shares the thinking that went on when she listened to her husband excitedly relate the news of the great new job he had landed working on a television show. He would be earning good money and he would also be working long hours for many months with fun people, going out for drinks after shoots, etc. She compares listening to him to feeling "like a woman being buried alive behind a brick wall." Each new bit of news: "brick, brick, brick." What is so stunning, so poignant, so relatable for many moms who give up their careers to stay home with their children? She said that even though she wants to scream in desperation about feeling trapped at home, buried by stress and isolation, she doesn't, she says, because she "should be grateful for simply being alive." She goes on to add, "But no matter how much I love him, no matter how thankful I am . . . I still watch the clock, waiting for Pat to walk in the door at the end of the day."

Resentment can also be a simmering flame that is slowly stoked over time by other sources of anger. *I am stuck doing all the shit work during the week in addition to my own job so that we can have fun family time on the weekends when he's home* is one sentiment I heard from multiple sources. *Why can't he give up that job and find another one nearer to home?* Or, to cite another example: *How can he leave me like this every Monday with so many responsibilities at home and with hardly any support from him? Sure, he's having a grand old time each week, but what about me? What about my career? My interests? Does he really have a clue how hard this is?* And perhaps the most damaging resentment of all: *Does he truly understand the impact this is having on the children?*

In the two stories that follow we meet super commuting couples who are wrestling with these real-life questions and challenges.

Faith and the housing market

I met Nicole soon after my family moved back to Minnesota and the seeds of this book were germinating in my mind. I knew a little about her situation and learned much more when we had a chance to sit down and discuss their experience. Her story is a good example of how the housing and job markets have been a catalyst for the increase in super commuters in this country and how quickly resentment can build when communication breaks down between partners.

Nicole and her husband Bryan met in Wisconsin eighteen years ago but currently live in Minnesota. They had been married for fourteen years prior to the chain of events that led to his accepting a position at a church four hours away in Wisconsin where his parents and sister live. At the time he was a pastor and she, a flight attendant for Northwest Airlines. They had discussed moving to Wisconsin then, while the kids were still young, but it was the summer of 2008, when the housing market was in the process of crashing.

Initially the move from Minnesota to Wisconsin seemed like no big deal. They were, after all, adjoining states (albeit big states) and in the meantime since Nicole worked for the airlines, Bryan was able to fly free of charge and use a family car when he landed. Their plan, as best laid plans tend to go, was for the family to move to Wisconsin by that Christmas or by spring of 2009 at the latest. Because of the wretched state of the housing market, however, they were unable to sell their home in Minnesota. Their only option then was for Bryan to continue to commute on a weekly and sometime bi-weekly basis between home and his job. As did many people back then, they assumed the market would turn around quickly and thus his super commute would be a temporary arrangement.

Two years later Northwest Airlines was merged with Delta. Since that meant fuller and fewer flights, and more time away from home for Nicole, Bryan now had to adjust his weekly schedule despite an increase in responsibilities at his church. He used to leave Saturday night and come back on Thursday afternoon. With Nicole flying more and with their children growing older and becoming more involved in school activities, Bryan now leaves his home in Minnesota either late Saturday afternoon or at three o'clock Sunday morning to drive to his job in Wisconsin, only to return to Minnesota Sunday night or Monday morning. On Tuesday he goes back to Wisconsin and then home again to Minnesota Thursday. Listening to Nicole relate the logistics of their daily life to me was mind-boggling even before I factored in Nicole's schedule which often involves international travel.

It should come as no surprise that the comings and goings of this couple trying to do what is best for themselves and for their children generated an unhealthy dose of resentment. A significant part of the conversation I had with Nicole revolved around the emotional struggle and pitfalls she was experiencing. She used words such as *frustrated, hated,* and *unhappy* to describe the first few years of the super commuting arrangement. She told me she had resigned herself to accept a move to Wisconsin as soon as they were able to do so (i.e., after they were able to sell their home in Minnesota) when he got the job as church pastor. She recognized the benefits in such a move, including the thrill of living in a new house, the kids living near relatives, and the fulfillment Bryan would find in his work. Plus, Wisconsin, like Minnesota, is a beautiful and family-friendly state.

But try as they might to get themselves and the children excited about a change in venue and lifestyle, they found as time dragged on that in fact they were stuck in limbo. Their daughter Amy is a competitive gymnast and her training center is one of the best in the country. Could they pull her out of a sport in which she excelled and a school where she was doing well academically? Clearly a move to another state would be disruptive to her and thus to her parents. And this was just one small slice of a very large pie filled with difficult challenges.

After another year passed in limbo, it became clear to everyone in the family that they would not be moving. If they were ever to experience the daily routine of a close-knit family, Bryan would need to look for a job back in Minnesota. He tried, but given the still weak job market and his specialized skills, he wasn't able to find one.

Nicole shared with me that especially at this point she began to feel resentful and angry and took it out on Bryan. "I wasn't very nice to him," she admitted. "Whenever we were together, there was a tension between us that I had felt before from time to time, but never like this. In my mind, it was a dark cloud hanging over our family and I felt trapped by our situation. We were both frustrated and I wasn't even sure how to talk about it. Who was I to complain if this is 'God's calling' for him? We had become emotionally as well as physically separated, and I had just about had it."

The resentment continued to build until it became blatantly obvious to their friends and neighbors. One day while out with some other couples, a close friend took Nicole aside and said in a low voice, "Look, I don't want to intrude, but what's up between you and Bryan? I feel uncomfortable about how you are talking. I know Bryan. He's a good man. And he loves you very much." Nicole hadn't realized that she had been repeatedly commenting that evening on how great her friend's husband was in front of everyone, including Bryan.

That simple observation served as a wake-up call to Nicole. She stepped back and realized that she was holding in the anger yet still expressing her frustration at how their lives were evolving as bitterness toward her husband. She looked at the greater picture and saw a need to re-evaluate where their relationship had come from, where it was today, and where it was heading.

"You are single or at least that's what it often feels like," she sighed. "Figuring all this out alone or with only token input from your partner is no easy matter."

Nicole told me that since they had always been a spiritual couple, she turned to prayer to help gain clarity and insight. She said Bryan's church prayed for them and that now, while their lives are still not ideal, she is at peace with where they are. She also spoke of the importance of having close friends or family who are willing to deliver the delicate yet important message of how one is behaving socially.

She also said that increasingly their relationship is returning to the way it was in the beginning of their marriage and that has helped to replace the resentment with love and understanding. When I followed up with Nicole several months later she shared that the long winter months had played on her emotions and that she was still feeling waves of "I've had it." But she also realized that for her as a social person, doing more and going out with friends made her feel better and more in control. Being isolated with just her kids, day in and day out without interruption and another adult to talk to, was just not the way to live life. Bryan has resumed his job search locally so they are waiting to see what the future might hold for them.

"All's well that ends well," the great bard once wrote. But not all super commuting couples are as fortunate in resolving resentment. Read on.

From the start

Patty and her husband Jim were college sweethearts and got married a few months prior to her graduation. During his last semester of college Jim was presented with a job opportunity that seemed too good to pass by, even though he was close to earning a college degree. The job involved working for a friend of his who had recently launched a company that installed underground utility cables. The pay was above and beyond what a typical college graduate could expect to make starting out, the hours were manageable, and on top of that he'd be working with a close friend. He thought the potential benefits for a job well done to be endless. The only problem was that the job was located more than four hours away by car.

As my conversation with Patty evolved, the mental image of their time together as a newly married couple appeared more like a revolving door and a blueprint for disappointment and resentment. Sadly, that image turned out to be correct, but it took a long time for Patty and Jim to realize what was happening. It started with Jim relocating that summer to the city where his job was based. That fall they were married and at the end of the calendar year, after she had finished college, she moved to join him. They were together in the same city for a few weeks but at the end of February he left home for his first big job with the company, a circumstance that was to occur frequently in the months to come. Typically he would be away four weeks at a crack and then back four days with his company paying for transportation to and from work. (You may wonder why I used the word *crack*. One definition is "break without coming fully apart", which is telling for this couple.) The arrangement went on like that for the first year, a duration that Patty described as not too bad despite being 22 years old in a new city away from friends and family. She worked two jobs and kept busy and since they were renting an apartment, she was free to pursue her own life and career goals without having to worry about fixing leaky faucets or shoveling the driveway after it snowed.

But that next winter came and as her loneliness intensified, they decided to relocate back to Minneapolis where they both had family and friends living close enough to them that they could drive up and help out on short notice. They had recently had a son together, and a year later, a daughter.

Patty stated that she was led to believe a few things that helped her hang on to their marriage despite fourteen years of watching her husband walk out the door for days or weeks on end. The first promise was that her husband's job required only limited travel; the second was that since his was a union position, there would be times where he would be technically unemployed due to the seasonal nature of the work and therefore off duty and free to be at home. Both promises proved to be dust in the wind. "Hope" is the word she used, not once but again and again. "When you are told at the end of a tough winter that 'I'm done, I won't do this next winter, I promise you,' you feel relieved and pacified. But nine months later, like clockwork, he's at it again, driving off into the sunset."

"I started to feel cold and I steeled my heart to guard against the pain and sadness that had become such a difficult part of my life," Patty confessed. "I tended to pull away from him on the weekends when he was home because I knew our time together was short and very soon I would be heartbroken all over again. Whenever I made mental notes of all the things I had to do in the weeks ahead because he was never home, the resentment began to build."

"The past five years in particular have gotten more and more difficult," she told me in a fit of frustration. "I don't know how much longer I can do it."

Lately, Patty has begun questioning whether Jim really *needs* to work back to back, out of town jobs. Her friends also ask her if this arrangement really is necessary, or does he do it by preference? Is it a way of avoiding the responsibilities of being a husband and father? Is their marriage in trouble? When she confronts her husband with these sorts of questions, he replies that if he quit this job, he would have to take a significant pay cut and then start climbing the corporate ladder all over again someplace else. "The money was the draw" was the reason Patty gave me for her husband choosing to leave college before earning his degree and to embark on a career that forced him to leave his wife and children on a continuous basis. "And it still is."

From November 2011 to August 2012, a total of nine months, Patty's husband was home for only six weeks. This was true even though he had started working closer to home and could now drive home Friday night and leave late Sunday afternoon. Ironically, Patty feels that this shorter super commute has actually added stress to their marriage because during the school year, she is put in the position of having to be the "bad cop" and enforcing homework and reading time on the weekends when he, in turn, wants to do fun things with the kids, a common sentiment among a number of moms I spoke with.

Although Patty admits that her husband calls home or goes on Skype almost every night he's away, Patty feels that increasingly his telephone calls seem more like an intrusion into the daily activities and study routines that she and her children have arranged together in his absence. It has come to the point, she says, that her children say to her "Can't he call when we're not so busy?" or "I really don't want to talk to him now." Patty's son and daughter are now nine and eight respectively, so for them, the way life is today is simply the way life always has been.

When her husband is home on the weekends, she said they often have a family movie night and he puts them to bed and tries his best to be both a loving father and husband. But lately, it just doesn't work the same as it did a year or two ago. Too much water has flowed under the bridge.

"Recently," Patty told me, "a neighborhood dad returned home unexpectedly early from an extended business trip. He hadn't yet gotten out of his car in the driveway when his kids burst through the front door and ran up to him, hugging him and jumping up and down with excitement. Dad was home!"

There was sadness and bitterness in Patty's voice as she related that incident to me. The unspoken trailer to what she said was that her own children do not acknowledge their father in that way—or in any sort of meaningful away—whenever he comes home. She didn't have to say anything further. The expression on her face spoke in clear imagery of the underlying reality that during the past decade Jim had super commuted himself out of his children's lives.

4

Following a Dream in Costa Rica

The purpose of life is to live it, to taste experience to the utmost, to reach out eagerly and without fear for newer and richer experience.
—Eleanor Roosevelt

Since her teenage years, Kate had a dream of living abroad, becoming fluent in another language, and helping people of various cultures see their commonalities rather than their differences. She had faced a fork in the road nearly twenty years earlier while getting her bachelor's degree in art. She met her future husband, Max, after committing to a year-abroad program in Italy, and ultimately had to choose between their relationship and Italy. She chose Max. They were married, and soon thereafter their first child was born.

Although her undergraduate degree was in art, Kate was also skilled in accounting and went on to have a successful career in business. Less free to travel and further removed from her love of the arts, Kate suffered the stress and challenge of living the "rat race." In the midst of that success and strife, an opportunity presented itself that seemed like "the chance to be the real me" and untangle herself from the choices she had made. She and her husband, who was also a business and construction professional, decided to buy land in Costa Rica and move there to work together on a "green building" resort project. For Kate, this project provided the perfect opportunity to combine her business acumen with her artistic flair, as she was involved in everything from landscape design to investor relations. They also planned to use a percentage of their proceeds to start a foundation sponsoring multiple community development projects.

And there were other benefits. Kate talked about the commonly held experience of "hitting the wall as a mom" and how meaningful her work became in helping her find personal fulfillment, which in turn resulted in more patience and reserves to be a good parent while helping the local community. Kate shared with me her belief in spiritual psychology, which in essence she described as living in higher consciousness and questioning the purpose of life. "The choices we make and how we serve the world are part of why we are here" is her fundamental life tenet and this belief drove her to pursue her dream of helping others in Costa Rica. That she could fulfill this meaningful goal while living with the family she loved was, to her, a divine gift.

Everything went well with their development plans, at first. Then the global financial markets collapsed and like so many couples caught up in the economic squeeze of 2007 to 2009, they were forced to take a hard look at their options. With their savings rapidly dwindling and the project falling apart, should they stay in Costa Rica, a place they loved and that had been their home for almost two years, or should they move back to the United States where finding suitable employment was tough, but not as tough as in Costa Rica? Kate had found other passions in Costa Rica, and wasn't ready to give them up, Wall Street collapse or not. She and Max decided that for them the only choice was for Max to return to consulting in the United States and for Kate to remain in Costa Rica.

They approached this new challenge as an adventure. "How can we stay together and make this work?" became the new question. They explained to their children, then 7 and 13, in a matter of fact way what would be happening and that they were taking a "wait and see" attitude to determine what might happen next. During the subsequent three and one-half years, they stressed the importance of supporting family members in following their dreams. She said that the kids understood that she had not yet realized her dream in Costa Rica and that their dad not only would not force her to move back to California, he would in fact do everything in his power to help her continue to pursue her goals. She felt strongly that what she said and how she said it gave her son the confidence to say later on that he wanted to move back to California and graduate from high school with his friends. And that's what he did. Max and their son lived in Orange County in Southern California while Kate and their daughter remained in Costa Rica for one and one-half more years.

Max super commuted between California and Costa Rica for nearly four years total, on a schedule that typically saw him working twenty days straight in the States and then having ten days off. Their home in Costa Rica was in a rural area that was a four-hour drive from the nearest airport and they often went as a family back and forth, combining the airport runs with major shopping escapades in the city. But this routine whittled Max's window of time to relax and be home with his family to eight days per month. After their son moved to California with his father, Max stayed there for five to six weeks before returning to Costa Rica for ten days, while leaving their son with family friends. School breaks were always spent together as a family, but sometimes three or four months passed before everyone in the family was reunited.

As is true for most super commuting families, the period of re-entry proved to be a struggle for the family for the first few days each time. Kate and her kids had established daily routines and when Max arrived touting a different parenting style, those routines were often thrown off track. These re-entry periods and the attendant parenting conflicts were the biggest sources of stress for Kate since they also evoked a strong sense of guilt around her being the reason why the family was separated in the first place. That being said, there is a positive side to the story: after sixteen years of marriage, their super commute had allowed them to rediscover their autonomy as well as their unconditional love for each other and for their children.

When I asked Kate what Max would regard as the "negatives" of his super commute, she replied, as had many before her, that parenting struggles and missing out on his children's milestones would be at the top of his list. Listed in the "positives" column would be the reduction in his daily commute that allows him more time to pursue hobbies, exercise, and relaxation, and developing a closer relationship with his son. This couple was one of the few who said they used Skype quite often while apart in addition to phone calls; and when they were back together, they made intimacy a priority as well as cultivating a quality social life together.

This story, of course, has multiple layers of change and challenge since it involves not only a super commute, but also an expatriation when the family moved from the United States to Costa Rica. When asked about resources in Costa Rica, Kate said that they were able to make friends with other expatriates in the area. However, the attitude of many of these expats was that they as a couple had chosen this arrangement and it was theirs to bear and therefore she was reluctant to share her frustrations with them. On the opposite end of the commuting spectrum, their friends in California reacted with more excitement and with expressions of how fortunate Kate and Max were. But they too often had little empathy for the difficulties inherent in a super commute saying, "How can you complain, Kate? You get to live in Costa Rica! And Max, you get to travel there and live in California!"

As was true of nearly all of the other interviewees, Kate answered no when I asked whether she would be inclined to join a group focused on the partners of super commuters if such a group existed. "I didn't feel I needed much emotional support during the commuting years," she explained. "In fact, the opposite was true. I felt more inner clarity and freedom than I had in years. If there had been such a group in my area, I might have volunteered to be a sponsor or something because I was always observing myself and keenly aware of how much commitment it took on my part to hold our marriage together and to see it prosper despite our being apart much of the time. There were definitely times when the Internet was down or we only had a few minutes to discuss critical matters, that we felt less like lovers and more like business partners. At such times, it would have been so easy to focus on the benefits of being separated and independent and just close our hearts and say 'it's over.' But because we had such a strong foundation to our relationship and we kept making plans for our future together, we just kept going. We had made this choice jointly, and my gratitude to Max for supporting me in it was always acknowledged—and appreciated beyond words, but we still had to be creative in our thinking and find ways to incorporate our 'new ways of being' into our marriage, instead of allowing them to break up our marriage."

And herein I think is found the difference between the couples for whom this works and those for whom it doesn't. Common themes in a successful super commuting relationship include maintaining communication and connection. Inherent in doing that is (a) respect for each other's dreams, (b) the willingness to think outside the box of a traditional relationship, and (c) the ability and flexibility to grasp the long-range goals of growing together as a couple.

Earlier I spoke of the shift that happened in the family life of Max and Kate when their son decided to move to California to be with his father. Another major shift occurred when Kate and her daughter decided to leave Costa Rica to allow their daughter to attend middle school in the United States. So how is the family faring today? Kate and her daughter moved to Santa Monica where Kate's family and many of her friends are located while Max remained where his work is in Orange County, about sixty miles away.

Why, you might ask, would they now choose to live apart if it's "only" sixty miles to work? There were two reasons. First, to bene-fit the kids. Their son still had one year of high school remaining, but Max and Kate did not want their daughter to attend an Orange County school because Santa Monica was where they ultimately wanted to settle and where many of their friends were located.

The other reason is the traffic in Southern California. Sixty miles can easily translate into a three-hour commute each way so Max has become one of the 233,000 super commuters in that region of California. He stays in a corporate apartment near his work, comes home to Santa Monica on the weekends, and often drives there one night for dinner during the week. Their decision to live this sort of lifestyle was once again based on not wanting to add daily commut-ing stress and on their continued commitment to supporting each other's goals and lifestyle preferences.

Reflecting back on their journey thus far, Kate shared that their attitude all along was "Why wouldn't we?" instead of "This will be impossible." Like Angela and Jacob in chapter five, they too were comfortable with letting go of traditional thinking about parenting and marriage, and adopting instead the view that "We are creators of our destinies and what works for us, works for us." They still hold onto some traditions as a family such as annual vacations with relatives, which Kate believes helps them strike a balance with the more non-traditional aspects of their lifestyle and of course, allows for quality time together. And finally, she stressed, "Always keep an open mind. After all these years of living and growing, we still don't know the full extent of our capabilities and potential. The possibili-ties are endless."

Knowing Kate as I now do, it would not surprise me if one of those "possibilities" were another year in Italy to pursue that dream of so many years ago.

5

The Best of Both Worlds?

*When making a decision of minor importance, I have always found
it advantageous to consider all the pros and cons. In vital matters,
however, such as the choice of a mate or a profession, the decision
should come from the unconscious, from somewhere within ourselves.
In the important decisions of personal life, we should be governed,
I think, by the deep inner needs of our nature.*
—Sigmund Freud

The purpose of this book in part is to examine how our culture and economy have influenced the rise of super commuting as a widespread—and in many cases, preferred—way of living and of managing a meaningful relationship. I personally have been judged, as have other participants in this book, when people learn that my husband and I made the conscious decision to have our family separated during the week. "How do you do that?" is often followed by "*Why* would you do that?" or the slightly self-righteous comment of, "I would never do that." But more and more people *are* doing that.

Consider the lifestyle of Angela and Jacob. Their story is an opportunity to showcase not only another variation of a super commuter couple, but also to share how the very definition of "being a couple" is continuing to change and evolve in our modern society.

Angela's divorce became final a decade ago when her daughters were ten and eleven years old. The reasons for that decision are complex and irrelevant to this discussion. What *is* relevant is her principle assertion, in retrospect, that her eighteen years of marriage represented an "antiquated" idea of a relationship. The terms of the divorce were traditional regarding the custody arrangement, and she and her ex-husband have had a fairly easy time maintaining a fluid back and forth with the girls, in part because they live only a half-mile from each other in Chicago. Her current "significant other," Jacob, lives nearly 1,000 miles away in Colorado and had been a long-time friend until well after Angela's divorce, at which point their relationship grew into something more serious. Despite that more intense relationship, Angela preferred living in Chicago. Especially when her daughters were young, relocating was not an option. Jacob, in turn, preferred living in Colorado, where the environment supports his passion for competitive cycling. Given these preferences, super commuting was and remains to this day an integral part of their relationship.

Angela's work is extremely flexible. In addition to building her practice as an executive coach and consultant, during the last several years she has been creating a software product and website that Jacob helped her develop. For the past three years, her practice has also included a corporate client in Colorado, so for at least one week a month, sometimes longer, she is there on site working. Between that client and the web development, she is able to spend a significant amount of time with Jacob. She felt justified in leaving her daughters with her ex-husband because this was her job. These were work trips and they were necessary to build her company. Besides, her daughters were used to their father not being around. When he and Angela were married, he was often away on business for weeks on end. Now that their parents were divorced, having their mother going away on business did not seem unusual at all. Besides, the girls were growing older and soon they were off to college on the West Coast. Although

Angela has now entered a new phase of her life, which allows for ultimate flexibility, she still chooses to live in Chicago.

During an interview with Angela I asked her what she considered to be the benefits of keeping her relationship with Jacob "as is," in other words, with neither one of them moving in with or closer to the other. She listed several advantages that were echoed by other interviewees I spoke with. One was that they both have plenty of time to pursue their own interests and grow as individuals without having to choose those personal interests over time as a couple. For example, since they usually know in advance when Angela will be flying to Colorado, Jacob schedules his most intense cycling for when she is home in Chicago. They both feel that the routine of separation and coming back together "keeps the relationship alive and meaningful."

The topic of sleep differences also came up during the interview. "Women want their own space," Angela asserted, and then said that she and Jacob have differing sleep habits and distinct preferences for how tidy they like the bedroom and its temperature. For her, sleeping alone when they are apart is not a bad thing. She went on to explain, "After my divorce, for the longest time I woke up asking myself how much longer I would be sleeping with an empty space next to me. But," she went on to say, "what's happened more recently is that when Jacob and I are sleeping together, he is moving closer and closer to me during the night, thereby interrupting my sleep and almost pushing me onto the nightstand! So you see, I'm fine with sleeping alone. I get a better night's rest, and that means I'm ready to take on whatever the morning brings, rather than starting the day groggy and cranky."

Since this preference for having one's own bed was lauded by many of those I talked to, I did some research on the subject and came across a *New York Times* article written by Bruce Feiler entitled "Married but Sleeping Alone." In this article he profiles a 2005 National Sleep Foundation Study that found 25 percent of

American couples sleeping in separate bedrooms, a trend that is gaining popularity in England and Japan as well. He also reported that the National Association of Home Builders is projecting that by 2015, sixty percent of custom homes will include two master bedrooms. The reasons for this trend seem to range from sleeping disorders (especially excessive snoring) to increased use of machines to treat sleep apnea, differing temperature preferences, the "early birds vs. night owls" personalities, and different work schedules. Many of the couples in this book echoed those same reasons.

Angela also has focused more on taking care of herself and told me that a recent solo trip to an Arizona wellness spa was one of the best vacations of her life because the sole focus was on what she needed to relax and reenergize. She also believes as a result of her independence that she doesn't have to compromise on much of anything, a sentiment echoed by Lori in chapter six who is also in a post-divorce, empty nest phase of life.

Their time together, however, has not been without challenges. She told me during an interview that included both of them that in the beginning, they struggled with what their relationship "should" look like to themselves and especially to other people. A shift for her came, "when I changed the definition of what I like in my life and what works for *me*. It was not an 'in your face' sort of attitude. It was simply coming to an understanding of what was right for me—and for us. After I reached that awareness, everything else fell into place."

Jacob shared Angela's insights, "Still being an individual when two people are living under the same roof 24/7 can be a real challenge," he said. "I suspect that most people fall short of their own expectations because of so many complex issues. And so Angela and I allow space to come between us from time to time so that we can both simply 'be'—as individuals and as a couple. For example, for days or weeks I don't have to multi-task *when* I'm eating, *what* I'm doing, *where* I need to go, or *how* I should react to her. We touch base often during those times, but in the interim I can plan my life according to *my* needs *totally* selfishly: my work, sleep, eating, cycling, whatever. And I get to do all of that without hurting her feelings. I'm fulfilled and she's not feeling neglected, and we continue to have a strong relationship and to care very much about each other."

Angela agreed, adding, "It's the same for me. I can hang out with a friend and Jacob doesn't care what time I come home. So that part is great. The downside, of course, is the cost of maintaining two homes. For us, the actual cost to commute is not too demanding. It's a four-hour door-to-door commute and the cost of flying between hub cities like Chicago and Denver is not unreasonable. I know many people who drive four hours each weekend to and from their lake cabin in Wisconsin. But we haven't decided on how our relationship will look going forward. We are together as a couple but that may continue to mean we are living apart. My kids are away at college so it *can* change. Before it couldn't, but now it can."

She glanced at Jacob, "Do you think that's scary?" she asked him.

Jacob paused a moment before answering, "In some ways, yes." He then said, "Whatever is coming, the changes will likely be significant. For instance, would we consolidate to one house?"

To which Angela replied, "Why on earth would we do that?"

To which all of us, including me, started laughing!

I then asked Angela, "Have you considered other options? You could get a smaller house or rent an apartment. Doing either of those things would involve less money and maintenance, while still giving you both your own space."

"Maybe." Jacob allowed, adding, "People often ask me, 'Does your relationship thrive *despite* the distance involved, or does it thrive *because* of the distance involved?' My answer is, perhaps a little of both. Making a dramatic change in our lifestyle for no real reason doesn't seem to suit either of us. I will admit, however," he said, stealing a glance at Angela, "that I find myself missing her more each time she leaves."

"Why do you think that is?" Angela asked him.

Jacob admitted he wasn't sure. Perhaps it was because he was getting older. Or perhaps it's because he was not training twenty hours a week at the moment. "When I'm training and working at the same time," he concluded, "I have little time or energy for much else."

Both Angela and Jacob have noticed emotional shifts during the eight years they have been together. For Angela, the moments of missing him are still there but are fewer and farther apart because, as she put it, "You simply get used to it. It becomes part of your relationship and your lifestyle. But what doesn't change is the excitement of seeing him again after we've been apart for a while. I still get super excited to see him." She gave Jacob a warm smile and continued, "I still get those butterflies in my stomach, as if I'm going out on a first date. Besides, in this electronic age of ours today we are never really apart. We use Skype a lot and we can enjoy a virtual meal together and talk about our day looking each other in the eye even though there is a thousand miles between us!"

"As a former married woman," she concluded on a serious note, "I believe that Jacob and I communicate with each other better than many people who live together day in and day out under the same roof. When we talk, it's usually for a reason. We actually have something to say to each other." She paused for a moment. "The downside is that you sometimes forget to tell each other stuff, making the fiber of the relationship a looser weave so to speak than a traditional relationship. You also might miss a physical cue that something could be wrong. For example, when Jacob was at my house recently I was feeling stressed out about work, something we all have to deal with from time to time. Jacob took me in his arms and kissed and hugged me until I relaxed. Simple things, I realize, but he had to be physically present to do them. Saying something to cheer me up over the phone or on Skype wouldn't have had the same impact."

I then asked Angela if she had noticed anything in her

discussions with her coaching clients that might support a trend toward "distant relationships"; super commuter or otherwise.

She answered that she had indeed observed a recent flurry of clients who are not happy in their current relationship. "It seems to me," she explained," that more and more people are feeling so alienated from their true self that they feel alone even when they are not alone. This can happen in any type of relationship, of course, but I am convinced it's far less likely to happen in a relationship such as ours because we are actively choosing this lifestyle. The only expectations for it are our own. Since it's a more dynamic and evolving lifestyle, it's harder to get into a rut."

Angela then told me about a friend's husband who has been out of work for six months. He has had opportunities to interview for incredible jobs but they have been located either out of the state or abroad. He hasn't interviewed for any of these positions because his wife doesn't want them to end up in a super commuter relationship. I wondered out loud how the stress of not having reliable monthly income compares to the stress of even a temporary super commute. "How is that impacting their relationship," I asked. "How is it impacting their children?"

Angela said that she has tried on several occasions to share the benefits of a super commuting arrangement with her friend; especially since one job was located where her friend's husband grew up and where he still has established ties. But it was to no avail. She didn't want to move and her reason was the children. She didn't want to be a single parent while her husband was potentially working on the other side of the world. But the reality is that the primary caregiver parent has hard days either way, whether his or her partner commutes two miles or two thousand miles.

Angela added, "Being in a super commuter relationship is about honesty and trust and overcoming one's own insecurities. It is also about balancing each other's needs with the needs of the relationship as a whole. The only 'right' way to be together is whatever works for two people as a couple, but you need to communicate about what that means to each of you." She went on to say, "People are afraid to balance their needs with that of the relationship and of letting go of society's rules about how it 'should' be or what it 'should' look like."

Jacob nodded in agreement. "A lot of guys I talk to claim to be envious of our relationship." he said. "They say things such as 'Wow, so you get to be with her *and* do your own thing *and* it's working out for you two?' I usually see genuine twinkles in their eyes—of admiration and envy, or a combination of both—although I don't see as much of that sort of thing in the eyes of women I talk with."

"Not one of my friends responds like that," Angela confirmed. "I have women friends who don't consider ours a valid relationship since we don't live under the same roof. It's 'just a phase' we're going through, they tell me, even though that 'phase' has now lasted eight years."

It would seem that many people are going through this same sort of "phase." Consider the topic of a *New York Times* article, "Unmarried Spouses Have a Way With Words," in which author Elizabeth Weil posed the difficult-to-answer question of what to call two people who act as if they are married but are not. And while not directly addressing a super commuter relationship, the website Unmarried.org is a wealth of statistics that highlight such trends as:

Over 12 million unmarried partners live together in 6,008,007 households.—U.S. Census Bureau. "American Community Survey: 2005–2007."

68% of divorced or widowed Americans plan to remain unmarried.—Gallup. 2006.

Nearly 40% of opposite-sex, unmarried American households include children.—U.S. Census Bureau. "America's Families and Living Arrangements: 2007."

"The definition of family is changing," Angela asserted. "How we define marriage, how we define a couple, it's all changing."

6

Trust, Infidelity, and Intuition

I'm not upset that you lied to me,
I'm upset that from now on I can't believe you.
—Friedrich Nietzsche

A silent thought running through most people's minds when they hear about a super commuter relationship relates to fidelity–or, to be more precise, *in*fidelity. It's the "when the cat's away the mice will play" syndrome and it's one that many people believe is inevitable in such a relationship. Part of the reason why is because that is what many people *want* to believe—it makes for juicy gossip and may vicariously add spice to one's life—and part of it is the perceived fallibility of Man (and Woman) when separated from a spouse for a long period of time.

When I put out the word via various social media outlets that I was seeking people to interview on this topic, Lori emailed me as follows: "Well my almost x (sic)-husband worked all over the world. He was routinely gone for two to six weeks at a time in the Middle East, Europe or South America. Unfortunately he met a young woman on one of these trips and began a four-year love affair." Then she wished me luck on my research. I of course immediately responded with an explanation about the book I was writing and how the readers of the book might benefit from her experience. She agreed to speak with me and as it turned out, she had a wealth of information to impart. Here is her story.

When we spoke, it had been seven months since Lori had left her husband and she had been processing the loss via her own writing. Lori and James each had prior marriages. He had been married twice and had a super commuter relationship with both ex-wives. Lori had been with her first husband for twenty-five years and after the divorce, had led a full life with family and friends living nearby, a nice home, and a successful professional career. James and Lori began a long distance relationship in which they pursued their own careers and interests while apart. When together they enjoyed a relationship that was "fresh and nice, a new experience each time." This long-distance romance went on for twelve years and during that time, James often suggested that she move to his city and that they marry and settle down together. Finally, she agreed. She sold her house, said goodbye to her family and friends, and drove off to a city where James was the only person she knew well. While she ultimately made friends and business connections in that new city, not having long-term relationships that allowed a lifestyle to slip back into comfortably whenever James was away made things difficult at times compared to the more fluid back and forth they experienced when living in separate cities.

After Lori finally agreed to marry James, things began to change and not necessarily for the better. Now that they were living together, she feared that when he was home he might feel pressure to spend time with her rather than do the things he enjoyed doing while she was living in her own home many miles away. For example, she would suggest that he finally do his taxes instead of spending the day at the movies. She also felt that things between them shifted because she was around most of the time and the "norm" was to be together, rather than being separated. Among other things lost as a result of living together was the reoccurring "newness" of their relationship and the excitement, both physical and emotional, that such novelty aroused. This phenomenon, of course, manifests itself over time in all marriages. The "newlywed" passion and excitement inevitably wear away over time and what's left, ideally, is the love and respect each has for the other that will continue to hold the marriage together until death do them part. Later chapters address the weekly or monthly re-entry transition and in them you will hear much more about this challenge from several other couples. Depending on how long the couple has been together prior to the start of a super commute, they might not have had the time together on a day-to-day basis to build a strong foundation for their relationship, and re-entry can come at a considerable cost.

As when James informed his wife that he had fallen in love with another woman.

It happened, Lori informed me, while James was traveling for his job several years earlier. She said he told her that being married "made him feel so tied down he needed to prove to himself that he could still do what he wanted." At this point in our conversation Lori addressed some of the crucial underpinnings that support any relationship, perhaps the most important of which is the integrity of the people involved. Also important, she believed, "is whether the person is an extrovert or an introvert and how they define their support system."

I found that to be an interesting observation and asked her to say more.

"An extrovert," she explained, "gets his energy from being around people. This connection to other people is extremely important and it needs to be an immediate connection, not one formed over a long distance. An extrovert needs people in his presence to get his juice." She went on to say, "It's different for an introvert. For an introvert, having time away to recharge is important and whether it's half the week or weeks at a time, he or she has more internal resources to deal with the challenges of being separated."

Lori went on to exclaim that a super commuting arrangement

"has the potential to be *perfect* for some people, whereas living together on a daily basis would be a mess." She brought up an issue that is often addressed in couple's therapy. When one or both members of the couple retire or there is an "empty nest" situation, conflict can sometimes arise from these major lifestyle changes. The amount of time together increases, routines change, the distraction of parenting is gone, and now the focus is back on the foundation of the relationship that exists between the couple. This foundation can be a blessing or a curse, depending on how well it has been maintained and supported over the years. Liz & David from chapter two half-jokingly told me how they have "teed up" an easy transition into retirement by having successfully cultivated lives both with and separate from the respective partner.

Another point she found worthy of note is a person's learning style. Is he or she visual, auditory, or physical/kinesthetic? Learning to identify these different styles and how each might impact relationships with people in your life both personally and professionally can help all couples when it comes to communication and connection, and may in fact help a couple decide if super commuting is the right decision for them and their relationship. For example, a "physical" learner is apt to find connection via a physical touch such as cuddling, kissing, or hugging. For such a person, extended time apart from a spouse might be more difficult than for other types of people. A visual learner, on the other hand, might be content to stay connected via Skype compared to an auditory learner who likely would prefer phone conversations while apart. As with personality, temperament, physical needs, and a need for independence, a person's learning style plays an important role in how one person relates to another and how likely a couple is to survive or perhaps even thrive in a super commuting relationship.

Despite the fact that James had cheated on his prior wives, Lori said she "had every reason to believe it would be different this time around." If she had to do it again, she thought that the one thing she would have done differently is to follow her intuition that he was having an affair. When she confronted him, he denied it, but later admitted to her that he had been in love for four years with another woman. He also admitted that he wanted to remain involved with *both* of them. Lori not surprisingly said that wasn't an option for her. Given his history of infidelity, she doesn't believe the super commute played a role in his propensity to cheat on her and said that he actually had a "local" affair when he cheated on his second wife. Distance is usually not a critical factor in determining whether or not an individual is inclined to cheat on a spouse or significant other. She laughed when she said, "James and I didn't have a communication problem. Except when it came to the lying."

The two did not have children together which Lori thought made her decision to end the marriage much easier, although she probably would have ended it even if children had been involved. She told me that in retrospect both her first marriage and her marriage to James have been learning experiences albeit painful ones. She puts up with less now when dating and is quick to be clear about what doesn't work for her. We discussed trust as a cornerstone of all relationships and how once it is compromised, things are often never the same again. It brings to mind a saying about couples therapy that I learned years ago while in training: "Yes plus no equals no" when it comes to a serious matter impacting a couple, whether that is a decision about having children, getting married, staying together as a couple after an affair, or entering into a super commuting relationship. If both people are not in complete agreement, but one of them choses to give in without fully exploring the implications of his or her decision, resentment often lingers in the background and it can sabotage the relationship down the road.

"Now I don't believe anything he says," Lori told me, referring to James's desire to stay with her despite his indiscretions, "Once trust goes, everything goes. And when that happens, it's best to let things be."

When a partner says one thing and then does another, that too erodes trust even when it's not related to adultery. In the case of Patty in chapter three, her biggest frustration was when her husband kept telling her, year after year, that he wouldn't take so many out-of-town jobs and yet continued to do so. It was a different kind of betrayal, but a betrayal nonetheless.

Up and down the coast

Maria's story profiled thirteen years of a super commuter relationship that took her and her family up and down the west coast. San Francisco to Los Angeles. San Diego to San Francisco. San Francisco to Los Angeles again. This game of leapfrog involved a pattern of her husband Marco staying at a job for a year or two only to get offered something bigger, better, more exciting in a different city. He would super commute and then later she and their three children would move and join him until another irresistible opportunity presented itself in yet another distant city. Then off he went on another super commute. Constantly living this way, back and forth, would appear disruptive to many people, but for Maria and her family it became a normal and perfectly acceptable way of life. She described it as a team effort between her and Marco, for the betterment of all concerned, including their children. The extra income and other perks made the sacrifices worthwhile.

When they first married she had a child from a previous marriage and they soon added two more children to their family. During this time she didn't work in corporate America; her full-time job was raising the kids and managing their home life so that Marco could focus on his skyrocketing career. At one point he accepted a job offer that meant he could finally stay put, at home, and they toasted to no more super commuting. But sure enough, a few months later he was offered a dream job in Los Angeles. The year was 2009 and Maria and the three kids were back in the Bay area of San Francisco where she had family and long-time friends,

the kids were enrolled in good schools, and their house was under-
water. Another move seemed out of the question. Since this was a
familiar dance, the couple decided they had no choice but to face
the music and resume a super commuting lifestyle. But this time,
Maria said, things began to quickly come undone.

In the past, Maria and the kids or Maria on her own had the freedom to visit Marco whenever he was living away from home. But
now that the kids were older and had homework and were involved
in sports, they had a daily rhythm that was similar to Patty's story
and they didn't want it constantly interrupted. Maria admitted
to me that looking back she kept herself so busy, she might have
missed or ignored Marco's attempts to get her to visit him in Los
Angeles more often. Not long after the dream job started, Maria
discovered that Marco was having an affair with a co-worker. After
ten years of marriage she and Marco separated and three years later
a divorce court decreed their marriage officially over. The irony is
that Maria and her sons had by now moved to the Los Angeles area
to make the custody arrangement easier and more equitable.

Maria described her husband as a 40-year-old intense individual
with a stressful, high profile job. The world he works in is fast-paced
and exciting and filled with young, single employees who are out
to work and play hard. Like many spouses who have experienced
infidelity, she said she never thought it would happen to them. They
were friends prior to getting married, had date nights, were excited
to see each other, talked and texted regularly, and always felt close
to each other whatever and whenever circumstances brought them
together. She told me she saw no warning signs but the more we
talked, the more I heard the similar sentiments of ambivalence that
I had heard repeatedly in my therapy practice. On the one hand
she felt lucky that his work allowed her to stay home with the kids,
yet on the other hand she would get upset at how hard it was being
a single mom to three kids during the week. She felt he resented
her parenting style, as it naturally tended to be her rules and her

schedules that were followed. She was in control of the household and he had to defer to her, however begrudgingly, because she *was* in control. So tensions mounted when he came home because he wanted to relax and do fun things with the kids, an inclination that is often referred to as the "Disney Dad" phenomenon. I discuss this dynamic in greater detail in chapter thirteen and it is a pitfall super commuter couples need to be aware of.

In hindsight, Maria shared that what she should have done is not agree to a super commuter relationship and instead find a way to accompany Marco each time he switched jobs. She said she also should have been more vigilant about their relationship and avoid getting in to the rut where things become messy and begin to sneak up on you. In what to many readers may seem like a minor point, she said she would not have agreed to shuttle Marco back and forth to the airport as she found this to be an inconvenient and annoying chore for her and the children to fit in to their weekly schedule. Other people who are in a super commuting relationship argue the opposite: that time in the car to or from the airport offered a chance for everyone to reconnect without the distractions of television and computers. She, like Nicole and so many others, felt that having family around was extremely helpful, both with logistical support and, more importantly, with emotional support once things in the marriage began to go awry.

People often ask me if a super commuter relationship runs a greater risk of infidelity than a traditional relationship. I think it's more accurate to say that a super commuter relationship, like any traditional relationship, can be susceptible to infidelity if the relationship is not nurtured on a consistent basis. It can never be taken for granted. The stories shared by Maria and Lori highlight the importance of communication with your partner, listening carefully to what each is saying to the other—or not saying, as in James's case. There are dozens of books in the marketplace on this topic and often the reasons cited for cheating focus on not feeling connected to, or valued by, one's partner. One of the best books about how and why affairs happen is *When Good People Have Affairs: Inside the Hearts and Minds of People In Two Relationships* by Mira Kirshenbaum. Clearly the amount of time and energy one has to spend on their relationship gets spread ever thinner as children are born, careers are launched or relaunched, and elderly parents are in need of care. As we go forward, we will meet several couples who have found ways to inoculate themselves against these "red flag" areas of stress that over time can chip away at the foundation of a couple's relationship.

7

Mom Won't Be Home for Dinner

The topic of working moms is a tap-dance recital in a minefield.
—Tina Fey, *Bossypants*

A generally accepted principle in super commuting is that most commuters are men. In my search for people to interview for this book, however, I had several women come forward who fit the bill in every way. What follows is a glimpse into what is involved when the mother is the super commuter.

There is a lot of talk these days about the so called "mommy wars" and all kinds of advice is bantered back and forth about what women should do to advance their professional careers. For some women, that may mean taking a job far from home because that is the best, and sometimes only, job they can find that conforms to their profession. Others make the choice to super commute for the betterment of the family as a whole; similar to the men we have met. Still other women put their careers on hold for that very same reason: to support her family by being available for them while her partner commutes.

Holly falls into the first category I mentioned above and her sons were six months old and five years old when she stepped off the plane in San Francisco to start her new job, a three-hour flight away from her home in Minnesota. A certified public accountant, Holly had worked in the airline industry for several years. She enjoyed her job but when the industry began downsizing and airlines merged into mega airlines, she saw the writing on the wall and took an early severance package in order to be home with her newborn son.

Life in Minnesota was full and going well when Holly received a telephone call asking her if she would be interested in an exciting new job opportunity. The only potential drawback was that the job was located in California. Having frequently traveled there for business in her previous position and generally liking the lifestyle there, she replied that she would be delighted to discuss the parameters of the job. Events moved quickly and before long she had an offer in hand. The job required her to be in her office near the San Francisco airport three days a week for three out of four weeks each month. The other days she was allowed to work from home. The job, the autonomy, and the salary all made her decision to accept the offer an easy one for her and for her husband, Tim.

When I asked Holly what people's reactions were to her super commuting with two small children at home, she replied that they were as you might expect: "How do you do it?" and "How hard is it on you and your family?" Her answers to those two questions bear consideration in this day and age when an increasing number of men are staying at home or being the primary caregiver either by choice, unemployment, or the wife being the "breadwinner" in the relationship.

As to logistics, Holly had a fairly easy direct flight from Minneapolis to San Francisco, followed by a quick shuttle ride to her office, which was near the airport and her hotel. She would typically arrive late Monday morning and work until midnight, which given the time difference meant that she was up nearly twenty-four hours that first day. Her personal goal was to work as much as she could while out of town to allow for family-filled weekends and more traditional business hours when working from home.

Like many people who work from home, Holly found the daily chores to be such a distraction she developed a schedule for what housework would be done when and by whom—including a house-keeper. The goal, she told me laughingly, "was just to keep up and to ensure that my husband and I have quality time that is not interrupted by laundry." They have no family nearby so she felt fortunate to live in a family-friendly neighborhood. One pair of neighbors became such good friends that they were asked to be godparents to their third child who was born after Holly had ended her super commute. She gratefully recalled the times when different families invited Tim and their children over for dinner when she was away in San Francisco. On one occasion, during an emergency, a neighbor tended to their younger son while her husband took their oldest son to urgent care. When I talk with people who have created or come upon situations like this, I am reminded of the phrase, "It takes a village to raise a child." In their case, the "village" includes the same daycare provider they have used since their oldest child was three months old.

Another theme that arises from the experience of Holly and her family is that of a husband comfortably assuming roles that are more traditionally female in nature. As Holly put it, "Tim was calmly and capably taking care of the children." For super commuters, knowing that the spouse at home is ready, willing, and able to do whatever is necessary for the welfare of the family helps them to work to their fullest potential while they are away from home. Holly's husband is employed, but because he has a flexible schedule, the two of them are able to share the logistics of childcare drop-off and pick-up, a stressful part of any day for many working parents. On those days when Holly was working and living in San Francisco, Tim often sent her photos of the daily goings-on at home, although he was careful about when to call her and what to talk about. She shared an instance where Tim was having a difficult time with the kids and called her in the middle of the night to vent his frustrations. From her hotel room two thousand miles away, there was little she could do and now they both were awake, frustrated and upset. After such an incident they agreed that Tim would not make such calls unless it truly was an emergency.

I often ask super commuting couples if they could start over, would they do things differently? Holly commented that were they to do it again, they would find ways to stay better connected during the week, such as using Skype rather than a telephone to communicate with the children. She also stressed that she would take better care of herself by working out more often in the hotel's gym, jogging when working at home, and getting more rest wherever she was. Perhaps the biggest thing she would change is getting to know San Francisco and enjoying its many attractions and world-class restaurants.

"It's not just a question of getting out of the hotel," she added. "It's more an issue of re-energizing yourself and feeling good about where you're living on a part-time basis. If you don't get out and about and take advantage of what's there, you likely will regret it later."

And how did her husband handle those two years as a Mr. Mom? Holly told me that one good decision for Tim was encouraging their oldest son to join a hockey league. That decision not only got them all on a routine and out of the house playing a sport their son enjoyed, it also allowed Tim to meet other parents, hockey dads in particular. As do women who stay at home, men grapple with the challenge of connecting with others and making new friends, and that can be difficult for a man because his role as Mr. Mom, while slowly growing in acceptance, is still not prevalent in our society. A post on the blog *The Art of Manliness* discussed the issue of "Making and Keeping Man Friendships" and when I came across it in December of 2012, it had twenty-eight comments from readers sharing their own tips and experiences navigating through these sometimes choppy, sometimes awkward, waters.

In accepting her position, Holly had committed to a minimum of twelve months on the job in San Francisco, and while she enjoyed both her colleagues and her work, she decided that after a year it was time to be back home with her family. She confessed to having mixed emotions on the day she gave notice, but when she received a phone call that her son had been diagnosed with multiple concussions and she was unable to book an immediate flight to Minneapolis, she knew she had made the right decision. She returned home and a unique chapter of their lives was closed.

She did add that in retrospect she would not want to trade the experience in San Francisco because it helped her and her husband to set their priorities and to grow in their marriage. It also gave Tim a hands-on lesson on what it's like to be the primary caregiver and to be a dad who is thoroughly involved in his children's daily activities. He has even more respect and appreciation for Holly as a mom and continues to support her career and what it takes for her to pursue her goals.

Holly also endorsed the sentiments of others that super commuting is not for everyone. "If you fundamentally need to be with your partner the majority of the time," she said, "super commuting is not for you, no matter what other decisions you make or actions you take. Either your relationship or your work performance will suffer, and probably both."

A short-term sacrifice for long-term safety
Another example of the father raising the children while the mother is super commuting came from my first interview, with a South African named Christian. Christian and his wife live in Johannesburg with their three boys aged 11 to 18. While his wife Rachel commutes to Cape Town for her job, Christian stays home to care for the kids and manage the household. Their arrangement has an end date of approximately two years, and according to Christian, is not that uncommon in South Africa. Many people there find themselves super commuting either because they live in remote areas with unemployment or, as is their case, they are trying to move to the city of Cape Town which is near the ocean and which he described as safer and holding more opportunities

than where they currently live. What *is* unusual is that he is the one staying at home.

"Culturally, Africans are 'real men,'" he said. "Most of them would describe an arrangement such as ours as a slow death. 'Man goes out hunting, wife stays at home', is the traditional scenario. Today that might translate to 'man works away, wife takes a position doing live-in domestic work, and grandma takes care of the kids.'"

When I asked him if he had found people to connect with or who could offer support, not surprisingly he said no. When I asked about other drawbacks related to his wife's commute, he replied that his wife would list at the top missing out on the boys growing up and he would also list his struggles being the single parent in a testosterone-filled house in a dangerous, stressful city. He offered music and the importance of routine as being helpful in managing stress and related anxiety as well as having dinner together every night. His wife reconnects with the family by planning "mom time" with her sons. Unfortunately, they sometimes view her attempts to bond with them as "interruptions" in their daily activities, a reaction that likely resonates with most parents of teens. Christian told me that because his children were not happy that their mother felt it necessary to leave home for work for days at a time, he often reminds them of what they have to gain once they move to Cape Town. As a family, he said they have moved several times to cities around the world and this quest for adventure is reflected in his advice for others: "Keep busy. Keep in touch. And look on the bright side. Such an arrangement can have benefits of new experiences, new skills, and more resilience. Someday soon we will look back and be glad we persevered."

These two stories profile the role of a mother in a super commuter household. As more and more women obtain high-ranking positions in the fields of medicine, law, business, and science, the dilemma of whether to enter into a super commuting relationship will arise more often than in previous years. A complex job market and expanding opportunities for both women and men to advance one's career will increasingly present themselves in locations far removed from home. In addition, many super commuters have shared with me the inherent benefit of being able to be solely focused on his or her job without the distractions and commitments of family life during the week.

In our modern society, it goes almost without saying that how relationships are forged and how they unfold is changing rapidly. Sometimes what one or both partners might want in the short term must be sacrificed for the long-term benefit of the family. Following is the story of a couple who speaks to this dynamic as well as to how the ramifications of super commuting may affect both partners, a mother with a career in particular.

Extreme parenting

Grace and Phillip have spent much of their married life apart because Phillip has been super commuting on and off for eleven years. His successful career in the medical device industry has evolved via a pathway that offered advancement and opportunity tied to changing jobs or positions. Often the promotion found him working in an out-of state office. Or, a non-compete agreement forced him to seek temporary placement far from home.

He started his first super commute when their oldest child was a baby. Eighteen months later, when their second child was only a week old, a new job opportunity presented itself that also required a super commute. Adding to the complexity of their family life these days is the fact that their third child has been diagnosed with a combination of Asperger's syndrome, bi-polar disorder, and Tourette syndrome. In addition, because his IQ is within the gifted range, he falls under the umbrella of a 2E child (twice-exceptional) and that too brings with it another set of challenges related to educational needs. There were several months while Phillip was commuting that they were in and out of the hospital and clinics trying to get an accurate diagnosis. What followed were months of appointments with neurologists, psychologists, psychiatrists, and occupational therapists. Since Phillip was away the majority of this time, it fell to Grace to do most of the therapy exercises with their son in addition to routine care for their two older children. She referred to what she was doing as "extreme parenting" and as such, she has chosen to put her career as a psychologist on hold. In her words: "Especially as one who works in a care-giving career, I need to be available to care for my family first."

Such medical challenges highlight how situations that most people choose to keep private in a traditional two-parent household become more transparent when one parent is far from home while the other is left behind to manage the household and raise the children. Phillip took two weeks off from work until their son was stabilized and he had to keep his employer constantly informed on his son's status. If he had worked in the same city as his family lived, and thus had a more normal daily commute to and from the office, it would have been much easier to rearrange his schedule each day in order to help out his wife and son with minimal impact on his job performance. As Grace put it, "Super commuting meant that he was all in at work or all in at home. There was no middle ground."

Which brings me to the point I mentioned earlier. While most everyone agrees that a super commute is challenging, an advantage Grace emphasizes is that Phillip being away during the week allows him the time and focus to excel at his career and earn good money and thus provide for his family. When he's home, he can afford to make family time a priority. She characterized his view of family time as centering on leisure and having fun, but she described herself as more strict. "When one has to run a tight ship," she said matter of fact, "it can be frustrating when your partner wants to suspend parental rules about bedtimes and dinner in order to 'connect' with the kids and make up for the time he is away."

"Phillip wants his time with us to be about fun," she added. "His commute has put him out of touch with the reality of the hard work it takes to maintain a home and family."

This statement shines a spotlight on how super commuter relationships have been described as similar to a divorce relationship in which the mom (traditionally) manages all the hard tasks such as homework and discipline while the dad gets to play and recreate during the weekend visitations with the kids. I will share more on this dynamic in later chapters but I mention it now for a reason. The stress around this very issue brought Phillip and Grace to couples therapy and Grace found the work they did together in therapy to be beneficial in helping "sort through our frustrations and soften the edges, refocus us as a couple, and return to our vows. It's tempting and often oh so easy to just throw in the towel. But when you consider why you chose to marry and how you work well as a team and have created a life together, you can find the strength to carry you through the rough spots we all face in life."

Grace also shared how losing her mother when she was 21 has influenced her perspectives on life. A mother of five, Grace's mom did it all while her husband, Grace's father, gave a lot of himself as an on-call physician in private practice. Remembering that life is short helps her to stay focused on the present and accept the reality of not working full time. But at the same time, she watches Phillip excel at his job and receive accolades while full time parenting provides so few external reinforcements. As a woman with an advanced professional degree, she has struggled both with pushing the pause button on her career and with what she described as the "urge to be productive and justify life" despite having her hands full as a mother and manager of a family in her husband's absence. In her own individual therapy she says she realized that "no one can be a 'supermom' forever and that there is no such thing as true balance in one's life. It's a myth. Working with a therapist helped me to hear that from an objective voice."

I have many "supermoms" come through my door and this phenomenon of trying to do everything and everything perfectly is not limited to the partners of super commuters. In the last chapter I offer three mottos for managing, if not avoiding, the inevitable stress and burnout that comes with the quest for perfection.

8

Easier Without Kids?

Let there be spaces in your togetherness
and let the winds of the heavens dance between you.
—Kahil Gibran

A common refrain of super commuting couples that have young children is how difficult parenting can be when a partner is away for much of the time. As we have heard, however, children might be directly influencing the decision to commute. For one family, a competitive sport in which their child excelled was one decision-making variable that led to the decision to live as a super commuter family for a time. For another, the high quality of schools their children were attending combined with the nearby support the wife's family members offered in her husband's absence were two key reasons for them to continue their super commuting regimen.

But what about those couples who don't have children, either by choice or because theirs are grown and have moved away? Allow me to introduce you to two couples who are in a super commuting relationship without the added strain of having to parent young children. At first blush you might assume that such an arrangement would be considerably easier. For Mary and her husband, both baby boomers living in Ohio, it does seem to hold true although ironically she moved in with her daughter at the outset of the super commute. In the example of Jeff and Robert, we witness not only how struggles over which partner is responsible for what exist even without kids, but also how a super commute led to a job change for one of them that ended up bringing them closer together as a couple.

An empty nester flies away

Statistics analyzed by the Rudin Center confirm that while the average age of a super commuter is under 29 years of age, baby boomers aged 55 and over are actually in the vanguard of the growing trend of super commuting in many parts of the United States, especially those who commute to Manhattan, Houston, or Minneapolis.

Why would a couple married for 32 years decide to start a super commuter relationship? To find out, I asked Mary who lives in Ohio why she made that choice at a time in life when most people are focused on retirement, not building a life alone in a new city. Her story is interesting in part because of a silver lining that manifested itself after she started working in a new and challenging job with a state agency in Columbus, two hours away from where she and her husband live. Mary, an empty nester, said she was ready for a change but not quite able to retire and thus this unique opportunity seemed like the perfect fit. Her husband was traveling more for his work and their kids were grown and on their own, but since they weren't sure how long she would want to work in Columbus, they decided not to sell their house and move. As it turned out, Mary's daughter also lived in Columbus, so she was able to live with her during the first year of the super commute.

Mary described the process of deciding whether or not to take this leap as one strongly influenced by input from her family. Her kids enthusiastically encouraged her to "go for it," her husband pointed out how her increased salary would help with their retirement goals, and a relative who is a counselor added his opinion that "it can work out however you want it to." After collecting all the feedback, Mary's excitement intensified.

"I see it as an adventure," she said in the same tone as many other super commuters we have met. "We initially thought I'd do it for a few years and then transition back to an administrative role closer to home. But I like the job and I feel that I am contributing something of value. So here I am, five years later, with no end in sight. It's working really well for us."

Another factor that made Mary's super commute so appealing? She is an only child and her father was ill and she knew she would be responsible of overseeing his care during his final years. His home in Cincinnati was a four-hour drive from Mary's house, but only two hours away from her apartment in Columbus. During this time she was able to travel there after work if needed and to alternate weekends between caring for her father and being home with her husband. She felt that living much closer to her father, a direct benefit resulting from her choice to super commute, was tremendously helpful in making his last year as comfortable as possible and much less stressful for her as she managed his subsequent transition from his home to an assisted living facility, organized his funeral, and handled the settling of his estate.

As more and more workers are faced with the dilemma of how to care for aging parents, I suspect that this dilemma will serve as another catalyst for people choosing to super commute, at least temporarily. A *New York Times* article published on January 17, 1999, was already hinting at this. "IN PERSON: A Survival Course for the Sandwich Generation," written by George James profiled journalist and nationally recognized expert on elder care Carol Abaya, who at one point commuted an hour each way to manage her parents' real estate company when both became incapacitated. Her subsequent challenges caring for her elderly parents combined with her inability to find sufficient support services motivated her to launch a magazine entitled *The Sandwich Generation*. For more than twenty years she has written and spoken about these crucial and sensitive topics.

Another surprising outcome of Mary's commute is an improvement in her personal health. She is able to walk to work daily and since she is cooking for only herself, she is able to follow a diet regimen that has enabled her to lose weight and to no longer require blood pressure medication. She has also discovered that living in a vibrant capital city has provided opportunities for her family to come together and to grow together. She and her daughter share a love of professional soccer and often attend games in Columbus. They have held extended family gatherings there as well due to the ease of logistics and entertainment options, and her husband's job sometimes brings him to town during the week, allowing them some extra time together while he is on the road for work.

Such unplanned or unexpected benefits speak to the importance of viewing a super commute as an option full of possibilities, not just challenges. You simply don't know what difficulties *or* opportunities may be in store for you when you decide to start something momentous or to shift strategy. In entrepreneurship this phenomenon is called the corridor principle. However detailed an entrepreneur's business plan may be, he or she rarely knows where their product(s) or services will sell best or what pitfalls they will encounter (i.e., what corridors they will go down) until the business is actually up and running. The same principle applies to starting a super commute.

Mary told me that several colleagues of hers also super commute in various forms. One of them has spent a year driving two hours each way to work, whereas several others have spent up to twenty years renting an apartment during the week and going home on weekends. I asked her if she felt in limbo about the life she left behind and she admitted that she did.

"There have been moments when I feel as though I'm missing out because I'm not there and seeing my friends," she confessed. "But I still participate in a weekly choir in my hometown, which is important to me. Ultimately this is my choice and I have had a supportive team here in Columbus that I have been able to lean on, especially during my dad's illness."

Interestingly, the colleague who referred me to Mary expressed a similar sentiment. This individual travels extensively for work and she shared with me a conversation she had had with a fellow super commuter, a pilot, about the disconnection they often felt from their "home" community. Both agreed that given the limited time they are home each week, less than forty-eight hours in some cases, there is little time to attend weekday social events, business community mixers, school activities, or other events where friends and neighbors tend to congregate and form friendships. In addition, intense workdays or business travel can also limit social connection and contribute to a feeling of isolation.

Mary estimates that retirement for her is three years away. When that day comes, she says, she and her husband will have to change some of the habits and routines each has developed during the past five years of her super commuting. "Otherwise," she chuckled, only half-kiddingly, "it's never going to work to be back in the same house. We don't have grandkids yet, but that would certainly be a factor in whether or not we someday move to Columbus where there is more to do and where our daughter lives."

Mary had some further thoughts to share. She was grateful that she had asked for feedback from those who would be directly impacted by her decision to super commute. She found them to be "possibility thinkers" who helped her think "out of the box" and thus consider both the pros and the cons of choosing this lifestyle.

"In weighing the balance," she said, "I believe that super commuting for someone my age offers a lot of advantages. It has certainly enriched my life and opened new worlds to my husband and me. The most noticeable benefit for us is that we have become much better communicators. We are more conscious of the importance of it. Two people can live in the same house and rarely talk to each other because outside commitments or routines get in the way or take priority. Just as in the saying 'you can't go home again', I had some initial concerns about whether my commuting would change things for us. But whether I commute or not, change will happen. It's the one constancy of life. If anything, I am more conscious of our relationship and I appreciate things more. And for those things that aren't working so well, we now take the time to understand why they aren't and try to find a new approach. In doing that, a new and better pathway is often revealed that otherwise we may never have taken or even known it existed."

Speaking of times when things are not working out well between couples, thus far we have heard several examples of the conflicts that often arise in a super commuter relationship that are centered around the stress of raising and nurturing children. This "division of labor" strife, however, is not limited solely to parenting. Super commuter couples without kids experience these sorts of conflicts as well. Jeff and Robert, together for eight years, had a similar story to relate and they do not have children.

Working together to be together
Jeff is a successful consultant sought out by clients from around the world to participate in projects, workshops, and keynote speaker appearances. When he and Robert started seeing each other, Jeff had a full-time job and traveled occasionally for work. Robert, in turn, had a demanding finance position at a large corporation. After a book authored by Jeff increased his speaker bookings, the daily chores of everyday life fell more and more on Robert's shoulders. Just as others had before him, Robert shared with me the frustrations that he and Jeff both experienced in their relationship. Essentially they had a choice: either spend their valuable, limited together time cleaning house and running errands, or dump all of the house maintenance duties on Robert, who was also pursuing his own career and building a social network of friends and colleagues. The tipping point came after Jeff was hired to consult on a yearlong

project in the Middle East that had him super commuting out of the country for two to five weeks at a stretch. As a same-sex couple, Robert and Jeff could not openly travel and stay together in that region. Religious and cultural restrictions forbade it. This reality led them to agree to a two-week stretch as the maximum length of time Jeff would be away at one time. And when he did return, they experienced the same "re-entry" challenges that heterosexual couples face.

Jeff chuckled when I asked him about his impressions of re-entry. He said that the biggest lesson he has learned is that "when I walk in the door, I am no longer a rock star. When I'm on the road I don't have to clean up after myself. People take me out to dinner and wine and dine me in grand style. At home I'm an average Joe—or rather, an average Jeff. I am Robert's partner and I need to do my fair share of housework and such. Sometimes it can take a while to shift back into domestic mode."

During the following year, Jeff's business grew to such an extent that he felt he needed to hire a business manager. That is when Robert spoke up and said, "If you're going to hire someone, why not hire me? With my business and legal background, I'm the perfect candidate." Juggling work, everyday life, and their life together had become almost unmanageable and financially, this did seem like the ideal solution. Although Robert stressed that it's rarely a good idea to work with the person you are romantically involved with, in their case it is working out fairly well. Jeff's business travels actually provide a healthy break in their relationship, an interim for each of them to pursue personal interests and gain perspective. Robert did confess, however, that he has taken some flak about his career change. Comments from former colleagues and other acquaintances run the gamut from old stereotypes surrounding gay men to the implication that he must have retired, since working from home does not really constitute "working." Such remarks notwithstanding, the two of them continue to office out of their home and they also have taken steps to lighten the load such as hiring a housekeeping company. As Jeff put it, "My hourly rate is a great deal more than what the cleaning company charges. To me, that is money well spent if it frees us up to work more or to have a more fulfilling personal life."

That said, they still have discussions around how things should be done. Like any other "single during the week" super commuter partner, Robert gets into a routine while Jeff is away and has his own way of doing things. Sometimes it's simply a matter of informing Jeff what those routines are, such as what time to walk the dogs, and sometimes it's a matter of schedules being tweaked. A priority that Robert has set for himself is to socialize with others whether or not Jeff can or wants to join him. He has discovered that waiting around to find out Jeff's schedule or see if he wants to go out when he gets home from a business trip was the source of his resentment.

"Now if Jeff is home and wants to join us, that's great," he told me. "If he'd rather be on his own and relax, that's great too!"

I asked Robert if he knew of others in a similar sort of commuter relationship. Although he was not aware of any exactly like his, he did say he is friends with people whose partners are a pilot and a musician in a band that often goes on tour. Just as other interviewees have shared, knowing other couples that have an understanding of this lifestyle, one where a person leaves often or for long periods of time for work, opens the door to commiserating about the ups and downs of having an absent partner.

"The concerns are the same," he said in conclusion, "whether or not you have children. Those sorts of parenting issues simply make the challenges of a super commuter relationship that much more challenging."

9

It's What You Sign Up For

If you don't like something, change it.
If you can't change it, change your attitude.
—Maya Angelou

s the super commuting phenomenon really that new? If you think about it, there are several careers where being away from home for weeks or months on end is simply part of the job description. Oil rig workers, long-distance truckers, pilots, and military personnel all fall under this umbrella. The entertainment industry is full of them: rock bands and their roadies who tour the country, the cast and crew shooting a movie in Vancouver for eight straight months, the list goes on. And then there are consultants and politicians and people who whose corporate sales territories stretch far and wide.

Why would people take a job like one of these? Perhaps it's the thrill of visiting new cities and meeting new people; or the constant change and challenges; or the salary; or the extra savings generated when day-to-day living expenses are covered while you're on the road; or pride in serving your country. Whatever the reason, what these types of jobs have in common is that the employee knows going into them that he or she will be required to be away from home for long periods of time. The primary questions that concerned me is how couples who live in this world manage to keep their relationships strong and what their experiences might teach other couples considering a super commuting relationship.

The military

Having counseled military families in my private practice, I have witnessed firsthand the strain that most families suffer when a husband or wife is called up for a tour of duty. When the prospect of my husband Ian being gone for days each week became a reality, I had a whole new level of appreciation, not to mention empathy, for how military families have to cope with a partner being gone for months or even years—and perhaps, on top of all that, be in harm's way. I met a local therapist named Carly whose husband, a National Guard reservist, had been deployed to Afghanistan for a year when their daughters were three and five. As she willingly shared her story with me over lunch, I asked for her insights into their experience. I also wanted to know what resources and support are available for military families and what if any of that information could be utilized for super commuting couples. Was it different for reservists compared to full-time military personnel? How did their experience differ living in the suburbs compared to another woman, Michelle, whose family moved from one Air Force base to another as her husband's orders dictated?

In my research for this book I interviewed members of three different military families. Carly's husband works in the field of technology and is a long-time reservist. Michelle's husband is in the Air Force and works primarily in an office on base except for seven months when he served in Iraq. Jason is presently a lieutenant commander in the Navy and his wife Teresa served as a Navy nurse for several years.

For the year that Carly's husband Kevin served overseas, Carly and her children ate dinner out of the house every chance they could, even if that meant bringing a picnic down to their neighborhood pool. Being away from the dining room table where the empty chair acted as a sad reminder of Kevin's absence was much easier for them. Carly told me that their youngest child had a particularly difficult time with her father's absence and tears at bedtime were a common occurrence. But as hard as that was, Carly admitted, it was even harder after Kevin returned home. His re-entry came with the stark realization that his family could and did get along quite well without him. As a result, Kevin became moody and depressed, and often got into arguments with his wife. Finally, a year after his return home he went to see a doctor and started taking medication for depression.

I asked Carly how much of Kevin's state of mind was related to what he had experienced overseas and how much to his re-entry. In reply, she said that his discontent had actually started the year before his deployment, soon after he had accepted a new job in a distant city and moved there for six months ahead of his wife and kids. Then, when he received his marching orders from the Army, he spent another six months preparing for his deployment. Although the family lived together during that time, Kevin had slowly disengaged from his family in the time leading up to his deployment date, seemingly absorbed in his own thoughts.

When his tour of duty in Afghanistan was over and he returned home, he felt estranged from the world that his wife and their two daughters had built for themselves. He didn't really know where he fit into their life anymore. She told me that looking back she should have done more to make him understand that she was proud of the sacrifices he had made and that he still played a pivotal role in their family's present and future life.

"At the time," she said, "it had just seemed easier to keep on with the status quo. Everything was working so well."

Having been raised to be a "strong woman," Carly was an independent sort and said she had relied on that independence to see her family through her husband's deployment overseas. But that same sense of independence created tension in their relationship after his tour of duty was over.

For many women I spoke with, the notion of "going solo" without their husband was often not an uncomfortable one. If it was, they soon learned that necessity makes the best teacher. The Army did not offer much emotional or logistical support for families left behind; there were no forums for spouses and children to discuss the nitty-gritty of daily life during deployment. As others I interviewed did, she reached out to friends for help and to the MOMS Club she belonged to. And she did respond to an inquiry from ADAPT, which stands for After Deployment: Adaptive Parenting Tools, a research project conducted at the University of Minnesota with support of the Minnesota National Guard that seeks to find ways to help families as they cope with the stress of deployment and reintegration (i.e., re-entry).

In contrast to Carly's experience, consider that of Michelle. I have known her and her husband Dan for more than twelve years, having met them when we played on a beach volleyball team together in Los Angeles. Teamwork turned to love for them and now they are married with two daughters. The family was living on an Air Force base in Hawaii when Dan was called up for a seven-month stint in Iraq.

I interviewed Michelle via emails and in every one of them she wrote to me I could sense the enthusiasm and pride she felt toward her husband. Their daughters were five and seven at the time Dan shipped out, and Michelle told me they took it pretty well.

"We showed them Iraq on the globe," Michelle wrote me, "and we explained how their father would be helping their country. The father or mother of some of their friends had already left for Iraq; others were about to. It seemed as though everyone on the base was supportive and sensitive to our emotions and fears so it was like an extended family affair. We were there for each other at all times."

She went on to say, "I remember my older daughter telling me, 'Mom, there are three bad things about Daddy being in Iraq: The first is I need help with the Wii. And I feel safer when he's home. Most of all, I miss him. But,' she added after a pause, 'there are three *good* things about Daddy being in Iraq: Sis and I get to sleep in your bed. And we get to go to Lunch Bunch at school. And most of all, he's helping our country."

When I asked Michelle how she felt about Dan's deployment, she answered quickly and forthrightly: "Well of course, the worst thing of any deployment is wondering if your husband will become a statistic. The best thing? That's easy. It's when he comes home safe and sound and you know your relationship is strong and can withstand anything."

"What about your husband?" I inquired. "What was best and worst for him?"

Again she did not hesitate. "For Dan, I would say the worst part was missing all of the major holidays, Student of the Quarter honors for both our daughters, our five-year-old turning six, teeth falling out, and all of those family events and milestones that lie at the heart of any close family's existence. The best for him was knowing that I am ready, willing, and able to take all this on without him, so that he could serve his country with a clear conscience and know that I had his back. Fundamentally, knowing that I love him and that I am his partner in every sense of the word."

In regard to whether she experienced any anxiety or depression during all of this she said, "No. Again, it's all about choices. I chose to marry a military man. Deployment is part of the package. I accepted the whole package. I kept busy with my girls and really wanted my husband to feel supported. I'm very proud of him. Imagine what it was like for him! He worked crazy hours and missed a lot of family activities."

In closing, when I asked Michelle if she had further advice for others who may be faced with a military super commute, or any sort of super commute, this was her answer: "While Dan was away, some things happened that were not particularly enjoyable to deal with on my own. But many people have it much worse than we did. Here's my advice: Suck it up. Everyone has a battle to fight. You can't choose everything that happens to you or around you. You can only choose how you react to what happens. You can spend your time complaining or feeling sorry for yourself or finding the negative; or you can choose to see the good and find something to be grateful for every day. Each night in our prayers I ask my daughters to find something for which they are grateful and then to thank God for that blessing. Find friends with similar interests so you can support each other. If I had to do it over, I wouldn't change a thing. I'm proud of my husband and I'm proud that he feels confident in my ability to take care of our children."

How do couples manage in situations where extended deployment is the norm? To find out, I interviewed Jason who has served in the Navy for twenty-one years. In the beginning his time away at sea fluctuated from five days to five weeks. Later, as his career developed as a weapons officer, the ships on which he served were deployed for up to eight months. For him, the hardest time was when both he and his wife Teresa were serving in the Navy. He had returned from a six-month stint at sea in December of 2003 only to learn that she was being mobilized as a Navy nurse to serve in Operation Desert Storm in Iraq. Eight weeks later she left for a five-month tour of duty.

I spoke to Teresa separately and she echoed much of what Jason shared.

As a result of such comings and goings, during the first three years of their marriage Jason and Teresa were together for a total of six months and even during those months it was tough. As a Navy nurse, Teresa often worked nights while Jason worked long days. Despite the many challenges they confronted, they have what they both agree is a close relationship and a strong marriage. Teresa did admit, however, that "For so long I felt like a single person who happened to be married and I leaned heavily on friends and family. I always said it was harder to be the person left behind and Jason disagreed until it came my turn to be deployed. Then he understood."

They now have two children under the age of five and prior to the birth of their oldest, Teresa transitioned out of the Navy and took a civilian job as a nurse. After their first daughter was born, she decided to stay home and for a while worked part-time as a lactation consultant. She is currently writing a book on the subject.

"She is truly amazing!" Jason proudly said of his wife. "When the kids are older and I have a more stable schedule, she will likely return to the academic side of nursing. She's a natural-born teacher! In the meantime she is home-schooling our children, which seems like a particularly daunting task to me, as well as tending to all the other details of family life when I'm away at sea. In all that time she has never expressed regret for any of the choices that she has made or that we have made together."

When asked about any post-Navy plans for them, Jason told me they have kept their options open. "Always being on call, always on the move, has made it hard to plan anything. It's safer to say that we *dream* about doing this and that when all this is over. Teresa has been so supportive of my career aspirations. I do know that as the kids grow older, my priorities are shifting. I joined the Navy twenty-one years ago at the lowest rank and now I am a lieutenant commander. I could be done anytime and be proud of my service to my country. I love the Navy and perhaps soon I will be offered command of my own ship. Of course, if I accept that honor, I will again be back at sea for extended periods of time. I will be super commuting again, as you describe it. And that reality gives me pause at this stage of my life. It's tough being away. And it can be tough coming home. It takes a while to get back into the groove of being a family. That can be a hard pill to swallow when all you have wanted for the last seven months is to be back with the ones you love the most."

In light of the above, I asked Jason if in hindsight he wished he had pursued a different career. "No," he replied without equivocation. "My path was chosen a long time ago and sometimes ignorance is bliss. In all honesty I am happy with the choices I have made. My sort of situation is not unique to the Navy or to military officers. Navy, Army, Air Force, Marines: we all go through the same kinds of processes and they sometimes deploy for much longer stints than I ever have. I would be remiss not to mention that. So in hindsight, what do I have at mid-life? I have a beautiful and loving wife, two wonderful children I love dearly, a good job doing what I believe in, and great friends at home and around the world. Why on earth would I want to change anything?"

The hidden cost of movie magic

Having lived in Los Angeles for eleven years prior to returning to Minneapolis, the entertainment industry is the one I am the most familiar with personally. For two and a half years I worked at 20th Century Fox as a C.P.A. while my husband has worked in the world of TV commercial production for more than twenty years. We have friends who work on television shows, commercials, and feature films, and their time away from home can vary from weeks to months. Even when the job involves local filming, there are still the fifteen-hour days when the actual shooting is done. The majority of our friends are not married but perhaps half of them are in committed relationships with someone who also works in the industry. None has children. Exactly why that is so is unknown, although part of the reason likely has to do with the fact that this lifestyle is hardly conducive to a Norman Rockwell-like family. To learn more about this phenomenon beyond my own personal experience, I interviewed Amy whose husband Alex works on feature films, television shows, and commercials.

Many people whose career is tied to the entertainment industry live a "freelance lifestyle." This means that whether they are a wardrobe stylist, a director, or a lowly production assistant, their employment ends when the job ends and they need to hustle to find the next one. Some positions are unionized, and those positions are highly coveted due to the perks they offer; but most positions are not. So, depending on your reputation, work ethic, or who you know, (it is Hollywood after all, people!) you may not find work for weeks at a time. This starting point of economic instability can mean a stressful lifestyle for some as they pursue their dreams. For others, long hours at work can lead to an office romance in which both members are in the "biz."

Two important goals I had in writing this book were to help super commuting couples, and, by extension, all couples, realize that they are not alone in their struggles and to offer insight and tips on how others have managed to navigate the difficult times in their relationships. The need for this book was reinforced in talking with Amy, a Los Angeles mother of four children aged seven, five, three, and one. Originally an L.A. native, she moved away to attend design school on the East Coast. She ended up working as a crew member on a television show and that is where she met her husband Alex, an ambitious, hard-working freelance unit production manager (UPM). Since Hollywood is where magic happens (right?) and since she was originally from the area, it made sense for them to move back to sunny Southern California where relatives living nearby would help foster an ideal family life for the couple. Or so they thought. As it turned out, even though Alex was a member of the Directors Guild of America (DGA) on the East Coast, the requirements for membership on the West Coast were more stringent and he needed many more hours of production experience before he could join the local DGA and work in Los Angeles. This meant that he had to keep taking jobs in such places as Boston, New York, North Carolina, and Georgia where he has contacts or where his contacts have contacts. This, in turn, means that he is typically away from home for weeks or months at a time depending on the job and its location.

As an interesting aside to this trend, the exodus of production out of California has been an ongoing problem for years due to such dis-incentives as the high cost of talent and state taxes. The harsh reality is that it costs millions of dollars less to film in a foreign country—whether that country is Canada or New Zealand—than it costs to stay in Hollywood, which for years was the Mecca of movie studios and the filming of television shows. In addition, many states have developed tax incentives to lure filming away from California, which boosts local revenue both directly from the shoot itself (hotels, dining, jobs for local crew and talent), as well as providing a steady flow of income long after the production leaves town in the form of sightseeing tours, memorabilia, and the like. For example, the company Chicago Film Tours offers a luxury motor coach tour of thirty sites in and around the Windy City where more than eighty movies have been filmed, including *The Dark Knight*, and *Ferris Bueller's Day Off*. And of course no trip to North Carolina would be complete without a $90 private *Dawson's Creek* boat tour!

How does this factor into our story, you ask? In theory, once Alex is qualified to accept production jobs in Los Angeles, he may find them to be few and far between. He will thus likely have to continue to commute long distance, and of course there is the inherent "freelance" aspect of his profession. When he and Amy first moved to Los Angeles, before they had children, his being away, according to Amy, was not a big deal.

"I thought at the time," she said, "that a little uncertainty in our life was healthy. It jazzed things up a bit. But now I want to know that someone is keeping track of how we pay for things and we are fulfilling our responsibilities. Alex would say the same thing and he hates leaving the kids for long periods of time. He misses them horribly. Jackson, our oldest, was just born when Alex left for a job in New York City. It seemed as though "family planning" for us meant scheduling our children's births around when Alex had to leave town for a new job."

Although Alex being gone for long periods of time is all their children have known, she told me he was devastated when he came home after leaving a six-month-old Jackson for a second time and

Jackson didn't remember who he was. But what would be worse than missing them, Amy acknowledges, is not being able to pay for their education and their extra-curricular activities.

"When Alex is between jobs" she went on, "he is very involved with the kids and their activities. When he's gone, he sees them on Skype and talks to them on the phone nearly every day. Recently, after being home and out of work for a year, he had to leave on a six-week job out of state. That was hard on the kids, for they had become accustomed to him picking them up after school and taking them to various activities. When they complain to me that they miss him, which is often these days, I talk to them about his work and why he has to travel so much. They understand, but still it's hard."

As mentioned, one of the reasons Amy and Alex decided to return to Los Angeles was because Amy's parents lived there and were willing to help out with the logistics involved in raising four kids under the age of eight. Although Amy loves having her children visit with their grandparents so often, there can be a downside to having relatives living nearby.

"My parents are not always accepting of Alex's career," she confessed, "nor do they always have much patience for the toddler years. I was the first of their own children to get married and have children and I don't think they were ready to be grandparents. They both still work and enjoy living an independent lifestyle, which includes having their house back in an adults-only status. I work with my mom, so she's more in tune with my needs than my dad is, but I don't rely on them to step in and offer help the way I would if Alex's parents were close by."

Amy was open with me about the strains this lifestyle has had on them. One source of stress, money, is common to most couples. As mentioned earlier, Alex's work, while demanding superior skills, is nonetheless considered a freelance type of job. When the job ends, Alex is unemployed until the next one comes along. Even when he is fortunate and a new job starts quickly, there is often a lag before his first paycheck arrives. As a union member he is eligible for benefits such as health insurance, but if a union member fails to work a designated number of days per year, those benefits lapse. Everything hinges on being employed and when you're not, bad things can happen.

"Alex was out of work for a year and during that time," Amy explained, "we lost our health insurance, we almost lost our house, and I lost much of my faith and trust in Alex. I went back to work, which I didn't want to do when the kids were young. But what choice did I have? I now work more than I did several years ago. My part-time job has become nearly full-time. It has become ominously clear that we *both* have to work to maintain a decent lifestyle and to guard against no income coming in if either of us was out of work. I'm an Interior Designer and my business has grown since Alex has been home. But when he's gone, how much time and effort I can focus on it is limited to the few days of nanny help we can barely afford, and even then my work suffers. I don't sleep well when Alex is gone because the kids don't sleep well when he's gone. I am more stressed about being a single parent and getting everything done, although I am less stressed about money because we have more of it when Alex is working."

When I asked her how they stay connected despite the ups and downs of careers, parenting, and lack of sleep, she said, "We try to talk every evening after the kids go to bed. The best part about our full days doing what we love is sharing the excitement and disappointments of it with each other. We are far more efficient with our time when we are separated because neither of us expects help from the other. We just get it done, period. It makes our conversation more focused on the positive things that have happened in our lives and less focused on the things we feel are missing. But there again, when Alex comes home, we don't always agree on how things should be done. But I'm an optimist, and so is Alex. Somehow we find a way to compromise and move on."

"So," I asked her, "how do you manage those times when frustration threatens to overwhelm that inbred optimism?"

"Mostly the way other people do," she said. "I got involved with Parent Education classes and a local MOMS Club, and spent time with friends and neighbors." Having grown up in the area, she has many friends still living in L.A., although one in particular has been a key source of support.

"She has close ties to the community and she grew up here too," Alex says of her friend. "She has rallied people to bring us food after the kids were born and when Alex is out of town. She is also my biggest fan in recommending my design services to others. It was a surprise that I met her during a chance encounter at a pre-school meeting, but knowing her as I do, I am not surprised she stepped up. She's the kind of person who would gladly mobilize an army to help out a friend. I am lucky to be her friend!"

"What is the primary goal for your future?" I asked.

"Ideally Alex will step up from being a unit production manager in charge of budgets to being a producer," Amy said. "That means that he would need to be on-set and out of town far less often. And once he qualifies for DGA West, he should find more consistent work closer to home."

During the last year when Alex was out of work, they made all sorts of "now that this seems done" plans, but Amy stressed that Alex loves what he does and could never put forth the same energy and sacrifice in any other line of work. "At the same time, it's hard being in a constant Catch-22 vise," she confessed. "As a working mom, and a single mom when Alex is away, I need to balance not only my family's needs but also *my* needs. I have to constantly keep all these balls in the air knowing that doing well in my own career is essential, given our month-to-month financial uncertainty. As hard as it may be at times, it's the life we signed up for."

10

Finding Balance: A Myth or a Necessity?

Forget trying to be Supermom—it's way too stressful and who needs more stress? Besides super heroes tend to wear a lot of clingy Lycra and none of us needs that.
—Alana Morales

In chapter seven Grace shared her thoughts about juggling all that is involved in being a mother and also the wife of a super commuter. In her opinion, the elusive goal of finding balance is a myth. The interview that follows shares a different view of that quest and highlights what Ann needed to do for herself in order not to succumb to the stress she was experiencing in struggling to fulfill both of these same roles.

Ann is a mother of two children, a successful physician's assistant, and wife of Ryan, a doctor who has been super commuting for the better part of fifteen years. As a therapist who specializes in working with high-achieving women and super commuter couples, I was struck by her conviction in this modern era to saying "no" to doing too much. Early on in their marriage, she and her husband were both investing in their careers something well beyond a forty-hour work week. Often it was double that. Much like Nicole and Bryan in chapter three, on a typical day their only physical contact was a passing kiss and a wave good-bye. They had two small children, finances were tight, and reflecting back she said, "That was a really stressful time, but we did what we had to do."

A job opportunity for her brought them the following year to North Carolina where her husband also found employment. Or so they assumed. The job Ryan had been promised failed to materialize and he ended up taking a position that had him traveling to a hospital in Washington, D.C. every Monday and back on Friday. Their kids were in elementary school, Ann was working full-time, her husband was gone, and so she decided to hire a college student to shuttle the kids to their afterschool activities. She just couldn't do it all by herself. But she was still doing everything to manage their lives, their home, and their family.

In February of 2006, Ryan was offered a new position in Chicago and that job also involved constant weekly travel despite initial promises to the contrary. On top of all that he had to start right away. That left Ann as a solo parent for several months until she and the kids could move and join him. The pressure finally became too much in June of 2006, when Ann was still working full-time, trying to sell their house, and packing up their belongings. Making matters worse, her daughter had developed seizures that hospitalized her, and Ann's boss didn't understand why she needed to take time off from work to be with her child. She described this mounting chaos as "the point when I hit rock bottom." Her advice to the partners of super commuters? "Find help, hire help, get help, even if it's only a few hours a month. It's just not worth going it alone. The effects on your mind and body can be devastating, not to mention the impact on your children."

Fortunately for Ann she was able to take a breather after they joined Ryan in Chicago. She took a few months off that summer to regroup, get settled, get healthy, and find a part-time job, which she loves. In her words, "I don't like doing things 'half-assed' and that is what was happening near the end before our move. I simply had too many balls in the air."

She also shared with me a common refrain of women today who

are relocating and trying to make new friends. Many of the women I have interviewed for this book are outgoing, energetic people who like having a strong social network (think back to Nicole in chapter three), but even for those women who wouldn't necessarily describe themselves in that manner, there is still a loneliness that seeps in when night after night you are the only adult in the house. When your spouse is a super commuter, and especially if you are not working, you can't capitalize on the social connections that tend to form with your or your partner's co-workers and their families. Although Ann does have a job, she rotates between different offices each day of the week, which also makes it difficult to forge meaningful office friendships. So while not necessarily in her comfort zone, she has made the effort to join groups like cycling and marathon training clubs with the two-fold purpose of participating in the outdoor activities she enjoys while at the same time putting herself in an environment where she can meet other people with common interests. Thus far it has been somewhat successful. She also told me that back in North Carolina she had lived in a large neighborhood development that housed many families with children the same age as her own. Living in the development was a god-send, she stressed, and her sentiment was echoed by many other women I interviewed.

Ann made an interesting comment when I asked her how their two children accepted this new life in Chicago—which really isn't new at all; it's how they have always lived. She said that they are doing fine but she hopes they will choose to live a simpler, less stressful life as adults. She also emphasized that despite the super commute—or perhaps because of it—time together as a family is very important to them, and that includes everything from planning annual vacations to sitting down to family dinners and just talking with each other.

She summed up her thoughts with, "Sometimes the simplest things are the best things."

Ann and Ryan will soon be celebrating their 25th wedding

anniversary and although there are no plans for him to stop commuting, she says she is comfortable with that decision since she frankly can't imagine having him around more often. She credits her own decision to keep working part-time, despite the opportunity to take on more hours and thus more pay, as a key part of her own self-care. Being home more allows her the flexibility and energy to better manage their lives. It also allows her to spend more time with the kids, to do all the little things and the big things that are the stuff both of memories and good mental health.

"I have found balance in my life," she said in conclusion, "and isn't that what we are all seeking?"

Time, energy, resources. If you think of them arranged as a triangle, these three factors form the base from which one can build resilience. But if one of the three is out of sync, you are off balance. If all three are out of sync, chances are you're flat on the ground, a position I suspect that many people can relate to. In the final chapter I offer three mottos to help strengthen your base—but keep in mind that this is an ongoing process. Think back to your childhood when you tried to balance a teeter-totter. Remember how much effort it took in the beginning? But once you positioned yourself near the center, small tweaks here and there were all that were necessary to keep it steady, although rarely perfectly or permanently balanced. That is how life often is. While it's important to strive for balance in what we do and how we live, at the same time we need to realize that we rarely achieve it. Good days will necessarily be mingled with not-so-good days. Nonetheless, if you can keep the base strong with friendships, eating well, and exercise, for example, it makes getting back to the middle that much easier on the difficult days.

Balance is something that each person needs to define for oneself, and if you are in a super commuting relationship, or soon to begin one, that definition may need to be periodically revisited by both partners. Shifting focus from outward, societal expectations to inward, personal needs and goals is perhaps the best place to start.

Navigating the Super Commute

11

Hello. Good-bye. Repeat.
Six Steps to Help Super Commuter Families
Cope with Ambiguous Loss

My relationship with him was defined by these complex emotions,
this mixture of gratitude and resentment.
—Otsuichi (*Zoo*)

Although support groups abound for "traditional" single parents, where does a super commuter couple turn to for support for a living situation in which a mom or dad is physically absent for repeated periods of time but is otherwise involved in the lives of the family? Similar to a divorced couple with children, this type of absence is called "ambiguous loss" and both couples and therapists may find the work of Dr. Pauline Boss helpful in managing the emotional challenges associated with a super commuter lifestyle. An expert in the field, Dr. Boss in her book *Loss, Trauma, and Resilience* (W.W. Norton, New York, 2006) identifies six guidelines for cultivating resiliency while living with ambiguous loss. They are:

Reconstructing Identity
Tempering Mastery
Finding Meaning
Normalizing Ambivalence
Revising Attachment
Discovering Hope

Each guideline is important, and although the descriptions may not correlate exactly with super commuter families, the overall emotions and processes involved certainly do apply. What follows is each guideline, how they apply to super commuter families, and my recommendations for ways those families can follow them.

For the first guideline of Reconstructing Identity, Dr. Boss recommends tasks such as revising gender and generational roles and identifying examples of resilience in one's own family. For example, think back in time to when you were surprised by accomplishing something difficult. How did you do it? Dr. Boss argues that we gain confidence when we have positive experiences with new people or in new situations, which in turn allows us to grow more confident in our abilities to cope with challenges in the future by recalling our success. Another example is choosing one's family values, as Angela and Jacob did in chapter five. Still another is when a family revises traditions whenever the commuter is away from home, the way Carly did. Because sitting at the table with an empty chair serving as a stark reminder of loss was simply too painful, Carly chose to have dinner with her girls outside of the house.

In our family for example, my sister lives with us and helps out as a surrogate parent and as added emotional support for me. Similarly, Maria's sister lived with her and her children while her husband was super commuting, although only for a few months while her sister was looking for a job. Nonetheless, that time together was precious to Maria. She greatly appreciated her sister's help with the kids, including her company over a glass of wine or decompressing together while watching television after the boys were tucked into bed.

Finally, as it relates to revising gender roles, the super commuter partner who is at home is playing both a traditional female and male role while the other is away. How much they choose to "take on" versus "hiring out" is up to the couple. Think back to Tim as the primary caregiver while Holly was away. He was managing most of what stereotypically falls to the mother, but he and Holly decided to hire a housekeeper a few days a month to ease the burden on both of them. Jan, who you'll meet in chapter thirteen, hired a handyman instead of getting upset when her husband has neither the time nor the interest to do those sorts of projects when his is home. The key piece to this process is to be accepting of those decisions however they may fit into the puzzle. Judging yourself around what you should or shouldn't do is not productive and I talk about the impact of this thorny word "should" in chapter fourteen.

The second guideline, Tempering Mastery, addresses the issue of control, or, more precisely, giving up control. Dr. Boss described this letting go of the need for absolute control, control being the very definition of mastery, as important because the more someone feels that he or she needs to be in control, the more stressed out they will become when the issues that created chaos or estrangement in the first place remain unresolved. It brings to mind the analogy of holding sand, as popularized by Kaleel Jamison in her book *The Nibble Theory and the Kernel of Power: A Book About Leadership, Self-Empowerment, and Personal Growth*. In essence, if you leave your hand open and loose, the sand remains. But as soon as you start to squeeze it and clamp it down, control it if you will, the sand runs out between your fingers. When one holds on too tight to anything—a relationship or a conviction, for example—you run the risk of it being smothered and disappearing.

For super commuter couples, such a loss can wear down the person left at home on multiple levels and lead to the sense of feeling constantly overwhelmed. On the one hand there is the unknown of when this super commuter lifestyle will end—or *if* it will end. And on the other hand are the inevitable controversies around parenting, the responsibilities for which fall heavily on one parent. Time management suggestions and learning tools for handling such stress can be very useful and served as the catalyst for my creating the support group I mentioned earlier. The idea is that women who are dealing with similar challenges day after day could connect and share their experiences and wisdom with each other, thereby imparting and receiving emotional and practical support. As Amy shared, she often found it hard to find people who can fully understand the struggles she and her family are confronting.

The gist of the guideline Finding Meaning is changing one's perception of a situation by shifting focus from the negative to the positive. We saw this first-hand in the accounts of Kate in Costa Rica and Christian from South Africa. While they both shared with me the challenges inherent in their daily lives, they both strongly expressed the attitude of "this is for the good of the family" and proceeded to turn a difficult situation into an adventure and growth opportunity—and, in the case of Kate, the pursuit of a dream.

Normalizing Ambivalence is about conflicted feelings. For example, a wife in a super commuter relationship might feel anger and frustration when having to deal with the daily struggles of solo parenting, while at the same time she looks forward to her husband leaving because that means that she and the children can return to their "normal" schedules and routines. The thing to keep in mind is that the presence of ambivalent feelings is not a problem per se; it only becomes a problem when it leads to feelings of depression or anxiety or increased tentativeness that in turn negatively impact one's daily life.

So how can we best manage such contradictory feelings? A place to start is to talk about them. Often in therapy the simple act of saying fears out loud diffuses them. Once released from rattling around in our minds they lose much of their power over us. Traditional coping skills, stress management techniques, exercise, or whatever you might list as an enjoyable activity could be considered self-care and help to lessen the presence or intensity of these feelings.

The fifth guideline, Revising Attachment, is about connecting in meaningful ways with others who are important to you. An important intervention advocated by Dr. Boss is to see others around you in your community as your family. As we know, it's all too easy to become isolated when the going gets rough. We convince ourselves that either people don't want to hear about our tales of woe or that their tales are worse than ours so we shouldn't complain. A common belief I hear in my practice is, "I should be able to figure it out on my own."

Today, with the help of social media, we are able to build systems of networks that were once thought unimaginable and that allow us to be in constant contact with friends and family. Carly from chapter nine had a lot to say about Facebook. As someone who at the time was new to social media, she now wishes she had been online when her husband was away because that would have helped her be more connected to important people in her life. She believes that having others bear witness to our lives is a very powerful expedient, and while it cannot replace having one's partner in close proximity, it is a valuable tool in building a meaningful and interactive community.

As nearly all the interviewees confirmed, connecting with and reaching out to neighbors was key for them. Asking for help with the kids or housework, spending time with friends the way Nicole in chapter three did, or joining a club the way Ann did in chapter ten, can help build a solid foundation of support for when rough times threaten to overwhelm you.

The final guideline of Dr. Boss's, Discovering Hope, is the cornerstone of Liz and David's relationship. Finding humor in difficult situations is their way of discovering hope because it helps them to cope and to draw closer to each other. For other couples I interviewed, discovering hope revolves around spirituality and their faith. For still others, it involves communicating with Nature which could be as simple as finding a few moments of quiet reflection in the woods. Kelly, for example, spends time with her horse that she refers to as her four-legged therapist. Last, but by no means least, Dr. Boss recommends developing more patience for yourself and others around you. Admittedly this is often easier said than done, but it is a valuable skill that can reduce stress and models this self-care for your loved ones.

Compassion is a very powerful emotion, wherever or to whomever it's applied—including to oneself. In the *Tao Te Ching: A New English Version* as translated by Stephen Mitchell, Lao Tzu, often considered the founder of Taoism, shared:

> "Simplicity, patience, compassion.
> These three are your greatest treasures.
> Simple in actions and thoughts,
> you return to the source of being.
> Patient with both friends and enemies,
> you accord with the way things are.
> Compassionate toward yourself,
> you reconcile all beings in the world."

12

How Do We Actually Do This?
Tips, Advice, and Strategies

This world is your best teacher. There is a lesson in everything.
There is a lesson in each experience. Learn it and become wise.
Every failure is a stepping stone to success. Every difficulty or
disappointment is a trial of your faith. Every unpleasant incident or
temptation is a test of your inner strength. Therefore nil desperandum.
March forward hero!
—Sivananda Saraswati

In the opening chapters of this book I mentioned that I would share advice on how best to manage a super commuter relationship as well as practical tips on everything from housing to logistics and helping the children stay connected to the commuting parent. This chapter embodies my experiences and suggestions, both professionally as a therapist and personally as a partner in a super commuter relationship. It also includes pearls of wisdom from the couples you have met in the book.

If you and your spouse are having the discussion of whether or not to launch into a super commuting arrangement, a hot button issue is likely to be money. I recommend the book *The Hard Questions* by Susan Piver to every client whether he or she is single or in a relationship. The chapters of this concise yet powerful book are divided into topics such as money, religion, and children, and each chapter includes several important questions that couples need to discuss and single people need to consider as they date potential partners. Her questions get straight to the heart of the issues that will cause conflict down the road if two people have differing opinions or beliefs about them.

For example, one question in the category of work is, "How do I need you to support my professional work goals?" For my husband and me, this was an important issue. Ian's job offer was a dream opportunity for him at the same time it was a critical choice financially for us. It led to further discussions about what kind of support I would need to avoid becoming resentful of his being gone all week and the additional responsibilities I would need to take on while he was living an "easier" life during his time away. We also discussed how he could help me continue to build my therapy practice and what projects we would hire help for. These conversations are on-going and we often revisit them when the need arises.

So what should your discussions include? The first and perhaps most important question to ask is whether taking a job that requires a super commute represents a short-term fix for an unemployment situation or does it support a long-term career move? Then, a related question: Is there a time frame for the super commute to end? For David in chapter two it could involve a lifetime. Christian's wife in chapter seven took the job knowing it would last eighteen months, after which time the family would join her in a safer city offering greater opportunities for them all. How you answer these questions may heavily influence whether or not you agree to a super commute, and if so, how best to manage it.

For us, because Ian's employer asked him to commit to at least one year, our first order of business was to reach out to everyone we knew in New York to seek their help in finding a suitable apartment for Ian to live in. Some of those people we only "knew" through friends of friends or colleagues via *LinkedIn* and *Facebook,* and sure enough that is how he found his first apartment. Despite what some people think about social media sites, they have proven to be invaluable to us during this journey. The sister of a former classmate of mine was the catalyst for finding the job Ian landed in Minneapolis and that was because I put out a mass email via my *LinkedIn* site. In addition, the majority of the interviewees I found for this book came to me from social media outlets. Friends and colleagues and people I only "know" through *LinkedIn* spread the word for me. Don't be afraid to ask others to help you, or as the author of *Zero to Zillionaire*, Chellie Campbell, calls it: to "send out your ships." Hers is a reference to the Middle Ages when kings would send their ships to the far ends of the earth and wait and see what treasures might come back. You never know what leads may return to you and enlisting others to help you out is great practice for those challenging days ahead when the need for some support will arise.

When people go through a tough time, looking back on it can provide some wisdom or strength to help them learn from their experiences and thus weather future struggles. This is certainly the case for Amy and Alex, the couple in Los Angeles we met in chapter nine. When I asked Amy what she would do differently if she could re-do the early years of Alex's super commuting, she replied, "I would be more aware of our financial needs and more involved in managing our expenses. I would be more in a "take charge" mode early on and less dependent on Alex's experience and insights regardless of his being fifteen years older than I." When I asked her if she had any words of advice to offer to others, she again gave a real-life answer.

"To be fair," she said, "there isn't much anyone could have told me going in that I would have listened to and adjusted our course as a result. I was young and felt invincible. We thought we could handle anything. I have learned so much about my tolerance and the strength of my character in the last decade that I couldn't wish any of it away. I do wish this last year had not been such a strain on our relationship, but without such lessons I wouldn't fully understand the breadth and depth of our relationship."

According to Amy there are a number of positives that can be gleaned from their journey. "It's the job Alex loves and it pays handsomely for its limited duration. Being able to work at something that you're good at and that you love, and earn great money while doing it, is really a dream come true." She went on to say, "One of the best parts about Alex super commuting is that I'm reminded of just how much I miss him when I can't talk to him during the day. When he's home and we are arguing, I hate second-guessing whether we love each other enough to make it work. When he's in the midst of filming, we will go a day or two without talking. I hate it. It makes me realize that when he's home, those moments of panic about money and the stability of our marriage are just that: moments of panic. Regardless of his commute, whether it's from the kitchen to the living room desk or from L.A. to New York City, I would miss him if I couldn't tell him about the anxieties or thrills of my day. In that way, I remember why we got married and why we keep struggling to make it all work. I need that wake-up call sometimes."

Managing stress

From my perspective as a super commuter partner, I am happy that my kids are seeing their mom do things without dad and that when mom needs a break, on the weekends when he is back at home, dad can also be a great primary caregiver. Ian and I have always shared the workload at home, from washing dishes to changing diapers. Not only has he been a big help with the kids, he loves to cook and do other household chores. Now that he is commuting to New York on a weekly basis, things have changed and this can be a source of frustration for me. The domestic chores now fall primarily to me in addition to school projects, activities for the kids, coordinating schedules, doctor appointments, in other words the whole parade of what it takes to be a parent of young children. Fortunately my sister who lives with us is able to step in and keep me from falling into the abyss. Nonetheless, the workload at home combined with my workload at the office can make for stressful times that likely would be mitigated if Ian were not super commuting.

Some schools of thought in the field of psychology, although not the way I practice, require a therapist to be a blank slate and not reveal themselves to their clients at all. As both a therapist and as the author of a book that is part autobiographical, that proves to be difficult, but to withhold some of the nitty-gritty, real-life struggles we have had seemed to defeat the purpose of the book.

This project started percolating one summer evening while I was on a date with my husband, who innocently asked me why I didn't blog about my experience as the partner of a super commuter. I was surprised he suggested it and asked him if he would be comfortable having our personal lives so out in the open. He replied that he would be as long as what I wrote about did not seep into the reality TV-type realm of revealing too much. Launching an initiative of this sort often involves a delicate act of walking the tightrope between providing helpful information to others and protecting one's privacy. It is certainly something I have had to traverse carefully in writing this book.

A recent disagreement between Ian and me offers a good insight into how stress can suddenly build for a super commuting couple. When Hurricane Sandy struck the Northeast in October of 2012, my husband was home with us. We were trying to change his plane ticket and figure out the most likely day he would be able to return to his job in New York. When I suggested he could be stuck in Minnesota for a week or more, he exclaimed, "A week? I'd be bored to death being here a whole week!"

Well, you could have heard a pin drop in the silence that followed that remark. I responded, "Bored? I'm so sorry that spending time with your family is boring for you."

The remainder of the evening passed by in quiet civility, but we had a long talk that night about several matters that had me exhausted and stressed out. To which he responded, "You should take better care of yourself."

Therein his statement lays the struggle for those of us left behind to do the "boring" work. It really *is* hard. I asked him which of the following tasks he'd like to take over to ease my load: homework with our daughter, managing our finances, compiling tax return documents, groceries and meal planning, laundry, doctor appointments, researching family vacations, his family's birthdays, their visits, Christmas, cleaning, getting up during the night multiple times with the kids, or booking his flights. And what about running my business and all that entails? He admitted he couldn't effectively take on many of those things, so I told him that the most helpful thing for me would be to get more uninterrupted sleep. Could he please help me with *that*? Yes, he could, and that started a routine on the weekends in which he gets up with the kids and I stay in bed until 8:30. He'll also make pancakes with them and take them for "dad time" so I can be alone to write or to work on projects, both for my business and our home.

The advice I want to pass along to readers at this point is to take a long and honest look at your triggers. What behaviors or words get you mad? What sends you over the edge? Is there a way to avoid them, or at least mitigate them? For those readers who can relate to this sort of struggle or to those therapists working with these types of clients (i.e., those stressed out by the demands of a super commuting relationship), one exercise is to ask what is commonly referred to as the Miracle Question: *If you woke up tomorrow and everything was the way you wanted it to be, what would that look like?* For some people it would mean the long-distance commuting and living apart would be over. For others it would mean having more help around the house or perhaps evenings out with friends. Whether your vision is great or small, can you pick one thing and simply do it without making excuses before giving it a try? For example, if your wish is to hire a cleaning company, you might dismiss it by assuming it's too expensive. But is it really too expensive? How much is your time worth? Instead of hiring someone on a weekly basis, perhaps you could hire someone once a month to do a thorough cleaning of high traffic areas such as the bathrooms and kitchen.

Other people have found that hiring a "mother's helper" helps them to stay sane. This could be a neighborhood kid looking to earn some money, a college student with a flexible schedule, or a retired woman whose own grandchildren live out of town. The goal here is to have someone else in the house to keep track of the kids while you spend an hour or two tackling a "to do" list. This strategy not only cuts down on the time necessary to get these things done, it also frees up time at night or in the morning for self-care or quality time with the kids. Often when both parents are working, whether in a super commuting relationship or not, many necessary tasks tend to be put off until the weekend, and the mad scramble to cram everything in and get things done leaves the whole family feeling worn out on Sunday evening and Monday morning.

One final tip I suggest for people feeling overwhelmed or stressed out is to practice not becoming attached to assumed outcomes. This may sound somewhat Buddhist in theory, but the reality is that when you set out in a super commuting relationship you have no way of knowing what good or bad will come of it, or how you and your family will grow and change as a result of it. The ability to be flexible is an asset that can impact everything and everyone, from the commuter's living situation to the kids' schedules.

Helping children cope with the commute

There is no right way to tell your kids that one of their parents is going to be living away from home during the week, so how you do it will depend on their ages and emotional maturity. It is important to stress the positives while acknowledging that they might feel sad or mad at times. For these kids, their parent is missing but isn't fully grieved as they can still have contact and their parent is still their parent, but a loss occurs nonetheless each time they leave. Here again is where the concept of ambiguous loss applies that I discuss in chapter eleven.

A parent's coming and going can be harder for younger children, as they don't easily grasp the concept of time. What worked well for Ian and me was having a monthly calendar on which we filled in different events. We drew a big heart on the day he was scheduled to return home; music class was every Wednesday, a visit from grandma was punctuated with an exclamation point, that sort of thing. Embedded in this strategy is routine. Routine is your ally and in the beginning you may need the structure of routine to see the family through the upheaval of transition. Your weekly routine might include a trip to the park every Tuesday and Thursday afternoon or a phone call with the commuter parent every night at 6 o'clock. Enlist people to help. Play dates with friends and letters from other extended family members all help children feel secure that the people they love are still very much in their lives.

Remember Christian in South Africa? He has three sons between the ages of 11 and 18 and all three were unhappy about their mother super commuting each week. Christian and his wife nonetheless emphasized that this temporary situation would lead to a new place to live that was safer, near the ocean, and financially better for the family. Remember though, that a four-year-old child may not have the emotional maturity to comprehend such benefits. The only thing that matters to him or her is that mommy or daddy is not at home. Nor do you necessarily want to raise concerns about the safety of where the family currently lives.

I was curious in particular about how the military might support the families left behind and so I asked Teresa and Jason from chapter nine if they had utilized any military resources while he was away. Teresa told me about several things that could easily be modified for super commuter families. The first was something called a Hug a Hero doll. It is a cotton stuffed pillow that on one side has a silkscreened photo of the parent dressed in military fatigues; on the other side the parent is dressed in civilian clothes. These dolls can depict anyone, not just military personnel. A mom, a dad, grandparent, anyone a child might be missing, and they are advertised as having "helped thousands of children cope with the stresses of separation." They have a "keepsake pocket" in which you can store a note or special item, and you can also add a feature that lets you record the person's voice.

Teresa shared with me a few other ideas, such as having a large glass jar filled with a chocolate kiss-shaped candy, one for every day the parent is away. Every afternoon the children are allowed to eat one candy "kiss" and watch the days disappear. The evening the last one is eaten involves a celebration, since everyone knows that the next day the parent will come home. A cautionary side-note Teresa added is that for some kids, this strategy can make things worse as it serves as a constant reminder during the week that their parent is gone. Like the phone call that interrupts homework, some kids prefer to connect with their parent on their own time, when they are emotionally prepared for it.

Another project is a "paper hug," which involves tracing the child's hands and cutting a length of string that equals their arm span. You tape one hand to each end of the string and now you have a paper hug that can be mailed to the parent or vice versa. Teresa said prior to Jason leaving, they all went to a Build-A-Bear work-shop and as a family they each made a teddy bear wearing the same outfit. On Father's Day, they sent Jason a pillowcase their three-year-old daughter had decorated. In our family, we found a book that allows you to record yourself reading the story. *Record a Story: Sesame Street Together at Heart*, is about a dad who has to travel for work and our son loves looking at it at bedtime and hearing his dad's voice reading the story to him.

Lodging and logistics

If your employer is not footing the bill for your weekly or monthly commute and/or lodging, you will need to get creative in order to preserve the financial benefit the job offers—which is likely why you accepted it in the first place. While it may sound glamorous to have a fancy apartment in Soho, the sky-high rent compared to other areas of New York, coupled with the likelihood that the commuter will spend most of their time at work or back home with family, makes renting that Soho apartment a less than optimal choice.

Since it may have been years since some readers have had to find an apartment, here are some suggestions for conducting a modern-day housing search online with websites such as Padmapper. com. This website pulls apartment listings from several other websites and consolidates your search into one location. It also lets you filter your search by price, number of bedrooms, type of lease, and listings that include photos. The "Super Secret Advanced Feature" allows you to add overlays that profile such things as mass transit stops, walk scores, and crime statistics for certain neighborhoods.

When answering an ad for a potential apartment, I first recommend setting up a new email address that does not include personal information. In this day and age you can't be too safe. It is also a good idea to compose a standard response for your initial email to a potential rental. That way you can save time by copying it into subsequent inquiries. When composing it, especially if you are looking to share an apartment with someone else, be sure to come across as benign as possible. Here is an example of a good inquiry:

I saw your listing for the apartment share in Park Slope. I am a manager at a mid-size firm and am looking for a quiet place as I work long hours and travel often. I am clean, responsible, don't smoke, am allergic to cats and for fun will grab dinner out or see a movie. I'd love to take a look at the place and could stop by tomorrow before work.

Such an inquiry should filter out places that failed to mention they have pets or roommates who party a lot; but if either of those things is something you are interested in, by all means mention it in your email. The critical point in your inquiry is to convey sufficient information to inform the landlord that you have a job and are responsible. Note that you aren't at this point disclosing details about what sort of work you do or your super commute. You can decide later if and when you want to do that, if at all. I also highly recommend seeing photos of the place before committing to look at it. One listing I found for Ian sounded great and so I requested pictures. The person sent a few of the apartment and one of himself—naked! Needless to say we quickly crossed that one off the list.

If you aren't sure you'll like the job or if it is a temporary position, you may want a month-to-month lease or switch to that basis after a year. After our first year of super commuting, we realized that Ian's apartment was great logistically but too expensive for the amount of time he was actually there, so he moved farther from his office and found a roommate to share the monthly expenses. As it turned out, neither the roommate nor the space proved to be a good fit for Ian. Fortunately, the lease on that apartment was on a month-to-month basis, and Ian was able to give notice and move into his own apartment across the street for only $100 more a month.

The art of flying

Airfare. It just keeps rising and if you are responsible for paying for your flights, it can be a huge expense. But take heart: here are some tricks to help you save money. Websites such as Yapta.com allow you to search for flights and then click on "Track price drops" for the tickets you are interested in. Whenever the fare changes, the website will email you. You can also select a target fare if you only want to be notified when a ticket drops below a certain price. Another website, Orbitz.com, will let you search up to three days before and after a given date to see if flying out first thing on Saturday morning, for example, is less expensive than leaving Friday night after work. Many websites also let you search all airports within a radius of a city, which can offer another way to save money. For example, when flying to New York, landing at LaGuardia can be cheaper than landing in Newark; however, you can take the train into Manhattan from Newark for substantially less than the cost of a cab from LaGuardia into New York. There are buses from LaGuardia that connect you to trains into Manhattan, but it might not be the most efficient option even at a lower cost. To state the obvious for anyone who has traveled to and from downtown New York, traffic to and from LaGuardia can be horrific and you don't want to be late for work!

These days nearly every airline has a frequent flier program, so see which one makes the most sense for you. Flyerguide.com is a good website for sorting through those programs in addition to offering general flying tips and information on specific airports. Some frequent flier programs allow a free checked bag but you then have to wait at baggage claim at the other end of each trip, not to mention running the risk of a lost suitcase. Traveling instead with only a carry-on bag and keeping a set of clothes in your work city can save you $50 or more per week by avoiding checked baggage fees. You can often accelerate mileage by signing up for a credit card affiliated with a preferred airline's frequent flier program, but if you do, make sure to find out what annual fees may be involved and if these fees seem appropriate. If you can earn a free ticket or two, $50 or even $100 a year might be a wise investment. And if you earn enough miles to qualify for upper level frequent flier status, you often are entitled to free upgrades, companion perks, early boarding, and other conveniences that help make those trips a little less frustrating.

Following are some additional ways Ian has learned to make his weekly back and forth commute between Minneapolis and New York a little easier both on a personal and a financial level. First, he applied for the Global Entry Card offered by many airports. It currently costs $100 and involves some paperwork and a brief face-to-face interview with a U.S. Customs official. Once approved, you are allowed to pass through a designated security checkpoint available only to cardholders. And you don't have to remove your shoes or take your laptop out of a bag. This may seem like a small matter on the surface but given the number of people flying these days, it can be a big time saver. In addition, when returning to the United States from a foreign country, cardholders simply scan their passport and fingerprint at a kiosk, make a customs declaration, and head off to baggage claim, thereby circumventing long re-entry lines. Another option at many airports is an "Expert Flyer" line at a designated security checkpoint. This line is intended for people who travel often and who are familiar with the routine of going through security efficiently. In other words, this line doesn't have families with young children juggling strollers, luggage, car seats, and diaper bags.

Next, one money-saving trick Ian has mastered is carrying a reusable water bottle that he fills up at a drinking fountain after passing through security. Since the average bottle of water costs $3.50 at an airport, he saves $7 a week or $350 per year assuming he flies fifty weeks a year, not to mention avoiding the huge environmental impact of all of those plastic bottles. The night before he leaves our house he makes two sandwiches that he eats while traveling and makes his own coffee that he drinks on the way to the airport, a few more simple ways to save a lot of money.

To make the flights a little more comfortable, he typically wears a jacket with a detachable liner jacket and several pockets in which he carries ear plugs, an eye mask, and lip balm. The outer jacket he rolls up and uses as a pillow and always picks a window seat near the front of the plane where it is usually less noisy and from where he can exit the plane more quickly when it arrives at the gate. He has invested in a Mophi battery case for his cell phone, a gadget that extends the life of the battery, which comes in handy when finding a charging outlet in the airport proves difficult. Since flight delays are common, having an iPad allows him to work, return emails, or read a book. And finally, to avoid costly cab fare and that aforementioned horrible traffic, when he lands at JFK he takes the AirTrain to Penn Station for $5 and then takes the subway to the office: $2.50 per ride or $50/month unlimited. (Fares are as of May 2013)

Some super commuters find that having their spouse and kids

drive them to and from the airport is a nice way for the family to connect with each other. Others find that the combination of time spent on the road, delays getting to the airport, poor road conditions in the winter, cost of gas, and kids' schedules makes it more expedient for the commuter to drive to the airport and park the car there for the workweek. Off-airport lots are typically less expensive than airport lots and many offer AAA discounts or frequent parker programs that help save money.

Finally, it's important to note that Ian's weekly flights give him the opportunity to engage in valuable networking with fellow super commuters and other business travelers. Some day he will be back living with us, but in the meantime he is making business contacts for possible future employment close to home as well as for his current company.

Staying connected

It goes without saying that a super commuting arrangement can strain a relationship, but thanks to modern technology there are ways that families can stay together despite being physically apart for long periods of time.

Photo post cards

New York City is filled with interesting people and things to see and my husband found a fun, easy way to share the city with us. He uses a smartphone app that allows him to upload a photograph taken with his phone and change it into a postcard. He can include a message and it is automatically mailed to our house. The kids love them and some favorites have been a view of the Statue of Liberty from the airplane and a series of different dogs he passed on his walk to work. It just takes him a minute and it helps him stay connected to his children. Remember . . . simple things can work magic!

Journals

Since a lot happens between Monday and Friday, having a place to jot down events can be a great way to keep the person who is away up to speed on the family's activities. Often by the time he or she returns, the stay-at-home parent can be mentally exhausted and not remember that baby Joe learned a new word or that Sue scored her first A in math. Keeping the journal in an area accessible to everyone, such as the kitchen, is one option. The kids can draw pictures in it after school or at mealtime, each family member can jot down something that happened during the day. You could also have each child and the stay-at-home partner keep a journal in their bedroom, making entries before going to sleep. And of course, the person who is away can keep one too, even if it's something as simple as using an online program like Wunderlist.com that allows you to have several different types of lists and share them with others. A change made to a list on your smartphone app will also be reflected on the website. For example, a list could be called "Dad's doings" and if he meets an interesting person that day he can type it as a line item on that list. Back home, the family can access dad's list online and see it updated in real time. Over the weekend they can all sit down together, review the lists, and talk about everyone's week.

Family calendar

Life is busy and finding a way to keep everyone updated on family member's comings and goings is key. In addition to journals, keeping an online calendar is an efficient way to do this. Several scheduling programs currently available on the market have features that allow access by multiple people and even a way to designate a person's event by color. It can be used to aid in the planning of family vacations, flight purchases, or any other happenings you don't want to miss or forget.

Skype and viber

Skype is changing the way people live and work, and best of all, it's free. You can access it from your computer, iPad, or smart phone, and it allows you to videoconference with people located around the world. You can also purchase low-fee plans and simply make telephone calls over it, which is a huge cost saver if your loved one is traveling to other countries. Viber allows you to make calls and send text messages anywhere in the world via Wi-fi or cell phone at no cost, other than your phone's regular data plan fees.

Family vacation super commuter style

"Stay-cation" is a new word used to describe a vacation in one's own local area. If it is in the budget, taking a family vacation to the commuter's work city can be a superb way for the family to bond. It allows every family member to get a real sense of what's involved in the super commuter's daily life away from home and see where dad or mom works. Having these experiences can help the family feel connected in the future. For example, dad might call one night and say, "Remember that pizza place we all went to? I ate dinner there tonight." The kids will immediately have a visual image of where dad was in addition to a nice memory of the family trip. Another benefit of such a trip: usually a super commuter is working such long hours that he or she does not have much opportunity to explore the city that serves as his weekday home. Having the family come to visit him provides such an opportunity.

Our children and I have taken multiple trips to visit Ian in New York City. Since we stay in his apartment, we don't have to pay for a hotel room and New York is an ideal vacation destination for us. It has allowed our kids to experience dad's life away from home by visiting his office and meeting co-workers, eating at his favorite restaurants, riding the subway, seeing the sights, and experiencing a culturally vibrant city. As Ian's relatives are predominantly living on the East Coast, it also has allowed all of us to visit with them more often than if he were not super commuting.

Whether your stay-cation is at home or in the commuter's city, contacting that state's tourism board is an easy way to discover what attractions may only be a short car or train ride away. Choosing to stay close to the family home means you avoid airfare for the whole family and as such, it might make it easier to afford a trip of longer duration. Also, check to see if there are "local" discounts to encourage residents to vacation near home. Some cruise lines offer such discounts to Florida residents, for example. And don't forget your clubs—and I'm not talking about golf clubs! The American Automobile Association (AAA) and stores such as Costco and Sam's Club typically offer member discounts for travel-related expenses such as hotel stays and admission to theme parks.

Therapy

As a therapist, I believe that both families who are in a super commuting arrangement, as well as those who are considering one, can benefit from a few therapy sessions. It could be the entire family discussing its concerns, or the couple, or the kids, or any individual member. I have plans to launch a support group for women whose partners are super commuting and its mission will be to serve as a source of encouragement and connection with others in similar situations. Although I realize that some people have an aversion to therapy, I would like to suggest that as with anything of this nature, finding the right therapist is key. Interview them as you would a doctor. Ask other people for recommendations. Google "therapist" and the name of your city. The website Psychologytoday.com is a popular one that allows you to search by criteria such as zip code or specialty. I then recommend calling a few therapists who you are interested in and ask them to describe a typical session. If you find one or two you think might work for you, book a session or better still, ask if they offer a free 30-minute consultation. When you meet with them, do you feel comfortable? Do you feel as though you could talk about anything? Do they cut you off to give their opinion or worse, do they try to tell you what you should do?

Some therapists accept insurance, some do not, and some can give you a receipt that you might be able to turn in for out-of-network provider reimbursement. Some clients use their health savings accounts (HSA) or flex spending accounts to pay for sessions. Others choose to pay with a credit card or personal check, avoiding the involvement of insurance companies altogether. If you chose to pay for the sessions with your health insurance, I always recommend making a call to your insurance provider or human resources department to determine your benefits and coverage. Another option that is unknown to many people is that some employers offer an Employee Assistance Program (EAP), the purpose of which is to help employees address personal issues that may impact their work performance. Many such programs include the option of short-term therapy and that benefit often extends to family members as well.

Therapy sessions offer a great, not to mention confidential, place to explore as a couple or individually, many of the topics discussed in this book. Your discussions might address issues such as co-parenting during separation, feelings of resentment and anger, managing stress, staying connected as a family, career challenges, feelings of depression and anxiety, or any of the items related to ambiguous loss. In the appendix I have included several questions to ask yourself and each other related to your relationship and the commute. While you could easily answer them on your own at home, they also are great tools to bring to therapy and explore in session.

13

Three Common Themes in Successful Super Commuter Relationships

You can kiss your family and friends good-bye and put miles between you, but at the same time you carry them with you in your heart, your mind, your stomach, because you do not just live in a world but a world lives in you.

—Frederick Buechner

As I reflect back on the process of writing this book, there are definite themes and common threads that appeared in many of the stories I recorded as well as in my own experience. If you are currently a super commuter couple or a couple who is contemplating this lifestyle, I urge you to carefully consider them. They are the key factors that will influence just how much you could learn and grow from such an experience.

Family

"It takes a village to raise a child." You have heard the phrase before and you have seen it evoked several times in this book. I agree it does often take a village to raise a child. Taking it one step further, the phrase could be modified to read, "A village helps to strengthen a super commuter family."

The importance of either living near family members willing to help, or in a kid-friendly community with neighbors willing and able to help, cannot be overstated. The less "village support" a stay-at-home spouse has, the more difficult it is for the couple to sustain and maintain a meaningful super commuting lifestyle due to the inherent burdens added by this arrangement that over time weigh on the family. In chapter six, Lori stated that the support of family living nearby can strengthen a relationship because it can "help keep life full" whenever the partner is away in addition to helping out with such immediate responsibilities as parenting and house maintenance. She shared that she knows of couples in other countries who only see each other once a month, but manage quite well courtesy of sympathetic and supportive relatives. "Having that kind of support is critical," she told me. "If you're just waiting around for your spouse to come home, it's difficult to maintain a meaningful connection—with your spouse or with anyone."

In chapter three Nicole described her neighborhood as extremely helpful as it organizes book clubs, block parties, and playgroups along with a wealth of other opportunities for neighbors to get to know each other better and bond over the "great unknown" that serves to define parenting. "Our culture doesn't easily allow us to simply ask for help," she observed. "Most people would rather hire someone they don't know all that well to babysit their child rather than to impose upon a trusted neighbor who likely would be thrilled to be asked."

Nearly all of the people I interviewed confirmed how critical family or neighbors are to making life more manageable for a super commuting couple and their children. Not having such support can be devastating to a family, as the following story illustrates.

Jan is originally from France, her husband Trygg is from Norway, and today they live in a remote mountain town north of Los Angeles. Their story highlights how vast cultural differences coupled with a super commuting relationship can put a strain on raising a family. In

2003, they met in California where she was working in the entertainment industry and he was serving as a pilot for private planes. Flash forward to 2012 when they have a five-year-old and a two-year-old and she is a stay-at-home mom. My interview with Jan was peppered with terms such as "tremendously difficult" and "downright impossible," and the reason quickly became apparent: The nature of Trygg's work had led to the decision to move the family to Norway by the end of the year "to allow for a sustainable marriage."

Jan touched on several factors that made this surprising decision their only choice. She first discussed the impact of geography. The town they live in is small and isolated and as such there are few sources of support for mothers of any sort, let alone "weekday widows" in a super commuting relationship. Living in a community where everyone essentially knew everyone else meant that friendships had a long history and there wasn't a need or interest to include an outsider. Most of her neighbors have partners with 9-to-5 jobs, or have family nearby, or were "locals." Jan often felt like an outcast even when she did attend La Leche or Mommy & Me groups. Adding to her difficulty in connecting with others was that few people could understand, for example, why Jan was unable to schedule outings or attend events with any reliability. But such was often the case. Not only is Trygg's job such that he is at the beck and call of clients, but he recently began flying to international destinations such as China. She also suspected that part of her feeling of isolation stemmed from what she perceived as a Southern California mentality of being strong and individualistic and figuring out solutions by oneself. This attitude stood in sharp contrast to Scandinavian countries such as Norway, which she described as offering a more communal and supportive social structure.

I was curious about her statement on cultural differences and found a paper that seemed to highlight this point. In 2004, the *Nordic Social-Statistical Committee* released "Single Parents in the Nordic Countries," and in it, profiled various Northern European countries' policies and views toward not only single parents, but also women in the workforce. It also emphasized how subsidies are offered by the State to encourage inclusion and equality among mothers, plus active participation by fathers during designated time-off periods from work. But for Jan and Trygg, the biggest draw for moving to Norway was that her husband's family was still living there.

When asked if she would do anything differently knowing what she knows now, Jan replied that wherever she and her family lived, it would be closer to family and in a bigger city where there are more opportunities for socializing and support, especially when her husband is super commuting. When asked if she had tips for other caregivers in a similar situation, she said that "thinking like a single parent" was helpful for her. She said a friend of hers, a single mother, suggested she read articles geared towards single parents. Soon Jan began utilizing skills and suggestions gleaned from them such as enlisting professionals to help in the home rather than waiting for her husband to repair something or start but not finish a project. In addition, she strongly recommended cultivating a net-work to help out when necessary. One example she gave was when her older son was stung by a yellow jacket and she needed some-one to help with her younger son while she took his brother to the emergency room. This is nearly the same scenario that Holly spoke of in chapter seven.

Another piece of advice she offered that might be easily applied to all parents of young children: "Make plans, but don't be married to them." She also found helpful tips in the book *Parenting for Peace: Raising the Next Generation of Peacemakers* by Marcy Axness, PhD, which includes suggestions for developing routines that are rhyth-mic on a daily, weekly, and seasonal basis as well as spending time in Nature and cooking healthy food.

"Lots of simplification helped, but parenting in these ways also takes a lot of time," Jan admitted. And so at the end of the day, Jan and Trygg concluded that the only choice that made sense for their family was to move around the world to be near family.

Our story

A source of tension between my husband and me is centered on vacations. Despite having a generous allowance of vacation days, Ian often continues to work on his days off, much to my dismay. In 2012 I lobbied successfully for a seven-day family vacation on a cruise ship. While the cost was more than we would normally have invested in a trip, my rationale for going ahead with it was simple: we would be together for an extended period of time that would permit us to decompress from the stresses in our lives and share quality time with our children. Best of all, there was no Internet or phone access available on the ship. Ian wouldn't be able to work! We therefore would have uninterrupted time together as a family to reconnect with each other and create new memories. In sum, I believed this trip was something that we simply could not afford *not* to do.

We had such a great time that we went again in 2013, but at the airport on the way home, the reality of our life in the real world smacked me in the face. After calling his office, Ian informed me that he needed to fly to South Africa for a job and that he would be gone for several weeks. After spending seven days of blissful time together, the keen disappointment of having Ian gone for three straight weekends, normally our family time together, left me feeling as depressed as our children, especially because we had a number of family events planned during those weekends. It was a stark reminder that his super commute was taking its toll on our time together as a family.

So what did I do? After a good night's rest I resorted to Plan B. I reminded myself of how strong our family ties are and how good life is for us all. Then I called my brother who lives a mile away to see if he would fill in for Ian as Katherine's partner at a local "daddy-daughter dance." Not only would he, he was honored to be asked!

I invited my sister to go with me to an annual charity gala that Ian and I were to attend together. She too was excited by the invitation! Finally, I asked my mom to stay with us a few days, and she accepted without a blink. I was so grateful for having been blessed with a family that cares and is so caring, even on short notice.

Following are several comments and observations on the importance of friends and family from the people we met in chapter nine.

Jason and Teresa

"Our neighbors were great in Virginia when I was gone. There were kids our daughter's age in the neighborhood and every evening the parents met out in the cul de sac while the kids played. They checked in on Teresa while I was gone to make sure she was okay. In addition, my in-laws are the greatest people on earth. They are always there for us. Whatever we needed, individually or as a family, they were there to help. I just can't say enough good things about them."

His wife Teresa added, "We never lived on a Navy base and so I learned how to make friends quickly. Having a network is so important whether that is through church, work, or family. The people I see struggling are ones who are more introverted and don't ask for help. They soon find themselves in a 'supermom' rut—overwhelmed, exhausted and lonely."

Michelle

"During my husband's deployment, we were very involved in our church and school, as were most of the families in our neighborhood. My closest friend's husband was also deployed. All of the other wives had already been through it, or were going through it with us. We lived on base in Hawaii, which is as far removed geographically from any continent as anything you can imagine. Our friends became our extended family and we had amazing support from them. People can choose to make friends and enjoy their help, or they can choose to isolate themselves. It was so rewarding to be able to return the support to these same friends when their spouses were deployed."

Amy and Alex

A common sentiment among interviewees is that many people don't have a network of friends and family who "get" how challenging this lifestyle can be at times, but I thought that because Amy lives in Los Angeles and Alex works in the entertainment industry there, she would have an easier time finding a support network to lean on. That wasn't the case. Amy revealed that, "While there are others who have a relationship like ours, no one really talks about it. I imagine there are lots of partners feeling the mix of emotions about their relationships: resentment and anger about not having job security, anxiety about money, understanding the desire to pursue what you love despite the costs. It would be nice to hear I am not the only one feeling like this and wondering how to make it work."

And although Amy and Alex have her parents living nearby, not having their unconditional backing made everything much more difficult. "My parents tend to judge our lifestyle and Alex's choices harshly. We can't rely on them in the way we had hoped and ours often remains an uphill battle. We are so grateful for the few close friends who have been there for us."

Re-entry

The re-entry period when a family is finally reunited after a few days or a few months apart can be a joyous one. It can also be a time of high stress and frustration.

Teresa and Carly both felt that when their husbands returned home, it proved to be a rough time for each of them. Teresa had hoped that after being apart from Jason for seven months while he was at sea, it would be easy and exciting to once again be a family, but what she found was that it took several weeks before they were able to regain the comfortable rhythms of their relationship.

Jason had only been home a short time before he sensed the many changes his wife had made to family routines. He had left their family life one way and after missing it and dreaming about it at sea for more than half of a year, he came back to parts of it being radically different, a common predicament, which calls into play the concept of ambiguous loss. Will family life and will each person's life be the same after the couple is reunited?

In addition, Teresa shared her observation that it is common for military couples to fight more as the date for deployment draws near. But this phenomenon is hardly exclusive to the military. As Liz also mentioned in chapter two, this sort of unconscious process of preparing oneself for a separation can be emotionally draining. Kelly shared that in the days leading up to her husband leaving he gets increasingly tense as he packs his bags for another four-week stint in Alaska, while she gets increasingly sad and annoyed as the day of departure nears.

You might remember that Michelle shared the following stance about her husband having to be away: "It's all about choices. I chose to marry a military man. Deployment is part of the package and I accepted the whole package." She went on to say, "It was interesting, though, when Dan returned from his deployment. I had heard stories of spouses having some conflicts as they re-align and re-establish the balance of power. I had spent seven months making all the decisions and taking care of everything. Even the dog wouldn't go out with Dan to get the mail because she wouldn't leave me. Fortunately he eased his way back in with slow but assured steps. Perhaps he had heard similar stories from his fellow soldiers and was being deliberately careful."

"Disney Dad" phenomenon

I mentioned this concept in chapter six and while the following definition describes a situation where a couple with children is divorced, a variation of it can sometimes apply to super commuter families.

The website Urban Dictionary.com has a lengthy definition of a Disney Dad, which includes:

"A father who doesn't have physical custody of his child. So, to compensate for this, he makes the visitation times with his child all about fun. The child's homework isn't done, there isn't a set bedtime and the child stays up late, the child watches all kinds of inappropriate movies/TV/video games. The father is more like a 'friend' that's a bad influence than a parent . . ."

Although most super commuter couples are not haggling over custody issues and in fact have strong marriages, the portion of the definition addressing conflicting parenting styles and dad's time at home being all about fun do reflect the frustration I heard from many interviewees. When a parent is reunited with their family for short periods of time, how does one acknowledge and balance the need for the family to have fun together with the realities of day-to-day living that are not fun? Unless "fun" and "reality" are carefully balanced, resentment is likely to settle in, especially for the stay-at-home spouse.

My best advice to super commuting couples is to ensure that parenting and all that parenting involves be constantly addressed and discussed and possibly re-defined as time goes on. There may be reasons for occasionally making exceptions to rules, but for the majority of the time, adherence to family rules co-created by *both* parents makes life easier and more manageable for everyone. When and how rules change will need to be an on-going topic of conversation between the parents and perhaps other family members who are acting as surrogate parents during the super commute.

Communication and connection

Is there not irony in the fact that our world today offers more ways to communicate, instantly, from nearly anywhere around the globe, and yet staying connected remains a problem for many couples? I believe most people would agree that this is so, and for many super commuting couples it is even more so. Having less time together face-to-face is a downside to this lifestyle and as such, figuring out what is your preferred way of staying connected, physically as well as emotionally, is critical. You likely will find that your preferences evolve over time and what works for adults may not work as effectively for children. What follows are comments and conclusions drawn from the interviewees.

Jason and Teresa
"I find the 'work-ups' to be the hardest," Teresa admitted, "the times when Jason is preparing for a long tour of duty and goes out to sea for days or weeks instead of months. Once he's gone, he's gone, but the coming and going in short bursts is tough on all of us. Just when we get used to him being away, he's back, but only for a short time. This is hard enough for a husband and wife, but when you add parenting and having to help the kids shift too, it's extra stressful. When Jason is home but in the work-up phase, you never know if he'll be late for dinner—or if he'll even be home for dinner. The kids are hungry so do you make them wait or do you make two meals? Do you mess up their bedtime routine to let them stay up until dad gets home? When Jason ships out, we tend to keep things low-key. We have friends over or we go out to eat. We follow a schedule and things run so much more smoothly. We plan events that give us all something to look forward to. Above all, we keep busy."

Having a spouse who also has a military background has served this couple well in understanding the realities of their jobs and as a direct extension, their lives. Teresa was a naval nurse for many years and her father was a police officer in addition to serving forty-one years as a Navy reservist. She knew the drill from early on.

In my own marriage, I had spent some time working as a production assistant on commercials and so I experienced first-hand what my husband's job entailed, including the crazy hours, the simultaneously boring and stressful aspects of it, and how he really could be too busy to take my phone call. Interestingly, a day after I moved in with him, he left for four weeks to work on a commercial shoot that took him across the United States. Our first go as a super commuter couple! Little did we know that ten years later his cross-country commutes to work and back would become a weekly occurrence.

Early on, in chapter two, we met Liz and her husband David. His nugget of advice? "Both people need to understand what life is like for the other person when you are apart. If you are able to remember that, it can help during those tough times when you want to start going down a list of complaints, upset about what your spouse hasn't been doing."

Carly from chapter nine shared a similar sentiment. She mentioned to me having read a magazine article that suggested an experiment in which couples pretend they are divorced for a few weeks. During that time the couple takes turns managing all the responsibilities related to home and children, and neither spouse can contact the other to ask for help. The ultimate goal of this exercise is to reveal what is important to them in a relationship, to see what each appreciates in the other, and to reflect on what that time apart was like. For example, what was life like as a single parent? Carly told me that while the concept at first glance sounded silly to her, she believes in retrospect that it can truly help super commuting couples. In her experience, until she returned to work full-time, she didn't fully understand why her husband didn't want to immediately spend time with the kids when he got home from his job.

"The shifting of gears when I went back to work was hard," she confessed. "I was exhausted in a different way than when I was a full-time mom at home. I also felt it was important that Kevin have the experience of being in charge when I went away for a few days with friends; but even so he doesn't quite get it. For example, whenever I leave for several days, I make sure that he has a list of important information and a schedule and some meals prepped and ready for the oven. When he last left for a weeklong trip with friends, he forgot to mention it to our daughters until I reminded him to do so. And there was certainly no pre-made lasagna in the fridge to help me out in his absence."

Carly's example highlights a difference in expectations that can go unspoken for years. Family life changes dramatically with the addition of kids and how a couple sorts out division of labor issues needs to be evaluated and re-evaluated until each partner is at least somewhat satisfied with how those duties are split up. This is especially true in a super commuting relationship. If one partner is gone for days and weeks at a time, what had worked prior to the start of the commute may no longer be relevant, and such issues as parenting, housework, and community involvement need to be brought back to the front burner.

Grace, a mom we met in chapter seven, added that she felt it is much harder for young couples to be in a super commuter relationship because they don't know themselves yet and the marriage is still trying to gain traction. Being separated as newlyweds for a long periods of time, the higher compensation and other benefits notwithstanding, can deal the marriage a devastating blow if this added strain is not acknowledged.

A final observation offered by Maria in chapter six was that after several months of therapy she realized that there might have been a few warning signs that their marriage was at risk. The first clue was that her husband Marco always wanted to work someplace else, as was evident in the multiple job changes and the displacements they required. She wondered if his childhood, which she described as being chaotic, contributed to his comfort with, and even desire for, constant upheaval. She also described him as spontaneous and impulsive which might be an asset in his chosen profession as an investment banker in the fast-paced technology industry, but less so when it comes to maintaining a strong relationship with a wife and children.

Maria's observations speak to the importance of knowing your partner's and your own preferred ways of communicating and staying connected. Were there warning signs in their communicating or lack thereof that neither Maria nor Marco picked up on, and that might have saved their marriage? It's hard to know for certain. As is often the case with divorce, one cannot always point to an exact cause and effect that led to the marriage unraveling, but as we have discovered in this book, it takes an extra vigilance to stay connected in a meaningful way during a long-distance relationship. You can take nothing for granted.

My interview with Lori in chapter six was one that stimulated some interesting side conversations that intertwined with the original topic of super commuter relationships. Key issues that could apply to all couples are those surrounding trust, personality, and styles of relating. She also made a comment about how for some people, not being physically together with their partner for much of the time can actually strengthen the relationship, a sentiment echoed by Anne in chapter ten.

When I speak to groups I often share the three mottos I have found helpful in conversations with clients and one is, "The 'should' shouldn't make you feel bad." I will elaborate on these mottos in the final chapter but briefly, the philosophy behind this motto is pertinent to a super commuter couple who might be thinking, "Maybe I should be missing my partner more" because many in our society have a hard time understanding why someone would chose a super commuting lifestyle even though the reasons underlying it are very complex. We learned about this reality first-hand from Mary, Angela, and Jacob. The notion that people can only be "close" if they are always physically near to each other is a false one for some people, as is the assumption that separation invites infidelity or the inverse ensures fidelity. The core lessons here are to trust your instincts and understand your needs and your limits.

David stressed that what is key for them as a couple is equally valuing their careers and their family time. If Liz notices that the scale is titling and he's spending too much time at work, she tells him so and often they will take a trip. Another perk he mentioned? Travel rewards. While business travel can be stressful, it also allows for many frequent flier miles and hotel points. To paraphrase, "When things get difficult, we try to stay optimistic and positive. Yes, our life is not traditional and it can be hard at times, but we also have a flexible schedule, enjoy nice vacations, and we aren't living the 'rat race' we would be had we stayed in Washington DC."

David and Liz wanted quality of life and this is how quality looks to them.

14

Three Mottos for Managing Stress and Fostering Resilience

*Some people believe holding on and hanging in there
are signs of great strength. However, there are times when it
takes much more strength to know when to let go and then do it.*

—Ann Landers

You may have heard the adage that things come in threes such as acts in plays or strikes in baseball. But the significance of the number three can be found everywhere in our everyday lives and across religions. Janet Bristow and Victoria Galo wrote *The Significance of Three*, which points out numerous groupings including mind, body, spirit; primary colors of red, yellow and blue; and verb tenses of past, present, and future. They also discuss how across cultures, "The number 3 stands for that which is solid, real, substantial, complete, and entire."

As I analyzed the common threads that run through the tapestry of this book, I was not surprised to find that there were three key themes. Nor should you be surprised that in this last chapter on the burgeoning phenomenon of super commuting, I offer one final trifecta. I have been a therapist for more than ten years and during that time I have heard common sentiments and concerns from clients and, prior to that, from colleagues during the five years I invested in the world of accounting. I have used that knowledge to formulate three mottos that I share with clients and also with audiences attending my speaking engagements.

In the interviews I conducted for this book I asked the stay-at-home partners if they felt the super commuting arrangement has impacted their own careers. As might be expected, the answers were across the board. Some said yes, others no, and for Grace, she reframed it as "I'm in a 'helping' profession but I need to help my family first." Many people confessed to not knowing what help they would need or assumed that they could accomplish just as much with their partner gone for most of the week and later found out they couldn't. In my own case I often feel overwhelmed either because I am spreading myself too thin between the demands of work and home, or I'm expecting too much of myself. Or both.

The definition of the word motto is "a short expression of a guiding principle," and although these three mottos were initially geared toward women, I believe that both men and women can benefit from implementing them into their daily lives. They are as follows:

1. Just because you can, doesn't mean you have to.

Several years ago I read a letter to an editor that has stayed with me ever since. A college student was commenting on a magazine article she had read that highlighted all of the opportunities women have today. She stated in so many words that, "We girls hear we can do anything and we interpret it to mean we have to do everything." And may I add to her comment that for many women, the need is to do everything *perfectly*.

How many of you have a hard time saying no? How many of you are running in five different directions at once? Or, like me, did you pursue a degree or career that you are good at but don't really enjoy? (I was a C.P.A. for five years before changing careers.) The phrase "Just because you can doesn't mean you have to" can be a powerful one for both children and adults when it comes to setting boundaries with people in our personal and professional lives.

For example, when someone puts you on the spot and asks if you can do something for him or her, a favorite response of mine is, "Can I think about that and get back to you?" In answering this way you aren't committing yourself on the spot and it gives you the opportunity to take a minute to determine if this is something you truly want to do *and* you have time to do it. Overextending yourself even with the best of intentions can become a self-fulfilling prophecy of, "I can't do it all perfectly." The fact is, you can't! And adding to the stress is the reality of how hard parenting can be, especially when your partner is away from home so often.

A perfect example is Anne in chapter ten who came to the realization that yes, she could work full-time, but that didn't mean that she had to accept the offer to do that. And so she didn't. Instead, she continues to work part-time and devotes the extra time she has each week to self-care and managing family life in a way that doesn't leave her drained and resentful. If you are in a super commuter relationship, you may find that you have to say no to some things or do them less often, whether that is volunteering at school or taking on a work project. It's okay to say no!

2. You can always change your mind.

This can be a scary one. For women, especially those with perfectionist tendencies, anything that might be interpreted, correctly or not, as "failing" is to be avoided at all costs. But at some point people decide that, for example, leaving the legal profession even though they have great credentials and a successful career under way, is a choice they have to make. First-hand accounts of this kind can be found on websites such as Women Leaving Medicine.com, on which female doctors post about their experiences of burnout, stress, and disillusionment with the field of medicine. The women's comments often reflect a common theme that while leaving medicine is a decision based on self-preservation, they nonetheless struggle with guilt when friends and family express their disbelief that someone could give up such a meaningful and lucrative career, especially after all those years of schooling and training.

When a career choice impacts a family, the stakes can be higher, but the cost of doing nothing, of remaining in a profession that for whatever reason is dragging you down, must also be carefully weighed. These kinds of deep discussions often lie at the heart of therapy sessions. Few situations are either black or white; there is normally a gray area involved and as you might expect, that gray area can make the decision process considerably more difficult, especially if you struggle with perfectionism. For someone who is afraid of making the "wrong" choice or of admitting that one they made didn't succeed in the way they planned, continuing to do well what you have learned to do well is easier than taking the risk of changing one's mind by changing careers.

Perfectionism or fear of failure is a common experience for women as well as for many men, and it can start early in life. Take a second and think about how you react when you make a mistake? What kind of self-talk or negative thinking do you engage in? When did that start? In junior high? In college? In addition to issues around control and wanting to please others, sometimes the fear of failure comes from thinking about what opportunity is lost if the wrong decision is made. As many of the interviewees have stated in this book, no matter which pathway you choose, you can't know what opportunities you'll find along the way until you start walking—or flying in the case of many super commuters. (Remember the corridor principle in chapter eight?) In Mary's story, for example, both she and her husband expected the commute to be a temporary one but then changed their minds and continued to do it. And as the interview progressed, we learned why Mary and her extended family were glad that she did.

In my talks to businesswomen I tell a personal story that high-lights this motto in another way. After I quit my international accounting job at 20th Century Fox, I decided to take a four-week floral design certification course, much to my parents' distress and confusion. "How could you give up a great job with benefits?" they wondered. The reason, bottom line, was that I was miserable working as a CPA. I initially thought after two years as an auditor at a public accounting firm that perhaps that area of accounting just was not for me and that somehow, magically, working in corporate accounting for a major movie studio in a city with sunny weather would be more appealing. Alas, that proved not to be the case. I became depressed and because I could not see a clear road to career advancement that was meaningful to me, at Fox or anywhere else, I quit without much of a plan. What I did know was that I have always enjoyed working with flowers and the thought of making beautiful arrangements for other people was intriguing, especially after five years of crunching numbers. I ended up landing a job at a small floral shop and guess what? It turns out I am a terrible florist. I needed to find another line of work, and while admitting I had "failed" was hard, I really had no choice. But all was not lost. Flash forward a few years to my wedding to when a silver lining appeared. Guess who was able to make her own bouquets, corsages, and table arrangements? Me! Were these creations subsequently featured on the cover of a Martha Stewart magazine? No, I can't claim that. But they did receive a number of nice compliments and we saved thou-sands of dollars.

Is there something at work or in your personal life that you really want to try, but are afraid to take the plunge? Do you automati-cally go into "all or nothing" mode meaning that you won't start something if you can't do it perfectly the first time? Sometimes just saying out loud, "What is the worst thing that can happen if I try?" deflates the fear and allows for some clarity in making decisions and moving forward.

For those of you contemplating a momentous decision such as a super commute, an exercise I do with clients when anxiety prevents them from making a decision or taking action is to write down all the things that could go wrong from making that choice. I then ask them to make another list of all the great things that could happen as a result of making that choice. Next we talk about each of those possible outcomes and what their fears are about them or the benefits that could arise. Which is more likely to happen, the bad or the good? Only time can tell, but in my experience, if the client goes ahead and does what he or she is hesitant about, but feels it is a good choice for them, the good usually ends up outweighing the bad. In other words, therapy has provided a safe place to express their concerns out loud and to brainstorm strategies for desired outcomes. Therapy sessions can also be an appropriate setting to practice responding to those people in one's life who may try to sabotage plans or make one question his or her decision, as in the case of the doctors I mentioned.

Putting your fears out on the table can provide valuable information and also serve as a way to identify resources you might not have realized were available to you. Simply put, getting out of your comfort zone expands your peripheral vision. You will certainly meet new people and who knows what other experiences might await you?

3. The *should* shouldn't make you feel bad.
We use the word "should" to indicate that something is the right thing to do. When I work with clients I pay attention to what words they use, especially if they are repeated. Often in sessions I hear the words "I should" used again and again in a self-deprecating voice. I *should* like my job. I *should* want to have more kids. After a while, that critical voice gets overly loud and begins to wear on one's self-esteem. I ask clients to take a moment to consider whose yardstick they are using to measure themselves with. Who says you

should? Our culture? Parents? Co-workers? You? In sessions, we often explore family rules ("family" in this case can be either one's biological or work family) in order to shed light on one's personal expectations. An example is a lawyer who has a promising career but is miserable in her work. Her dad is a lawyer, her sister is a lawyer, and the family "rule" is she too should be a lawyer. In a very real sense this poor woman was dragged kicking and screaming (albeit silently) into her career. The first motto also could be applied here: Just because she has the ability to become a lawyer doesn't mean she has to follow that career path.

Offshoots of the "should" issue may apply to the parent who stays at home to care for young children and/or aging parents. Some super commuter couples might decide it makes sense for the partner at home to only work part-time or to suspend his or her career. A few points to weigh against that relate to feelings of grief about the loss of one's professional identity, a sense of isolation especially during the toddler years, and issues surrounding money now that there is only one income. Finding other stay-at-home parents with similar backgrounds and interests to connect with can be another difficult challenge depending on where you live. And as the partner in a super commuter relationship, you now have your main source of support gone on a regular basis.

If you recall, chapter three discusses feelings of resentment. In it, Patty mentions feeling guilt about wanting to continue to work and the impact of her working on her kids. The guilt she talks about is something I think most mothers can relate to whether or not their partner is a super commuter. How to be a "supermom" to the maximum benefit of all is the question and frankly, I feel the answer is, you can't. Consider that first motto *just because you can, doesn't mean you have to*. Patty can stay at home but she doesn't have to. She has chosen instead to pursue a career that fulfills her and connects her to fellow colleagues. I often talk about this in the context of women who try to do too much. Just because you *can* join another committee or you *can* add a day of carpool, do you really have to? Do you have the stamina and time in your day to take on something additional? Or, if by doing those things, will that take away from what you give to other commitments in your life, including taking time for yourself?

Patty also touched on some of the "shoulds" that pop up in her life while we were discussing the cycle of negative "self-talk" she catches herself engaging in at times. She knew she *should* ask for help from those around her but she is loathe doing so and believes that if her spouse were not super commuting, she wouldn't need to ask for help. She also knows it would be beneficial for her to do more things for herself such as a girls' night out each month, but at the same time she wants to be around for her family and *should* be building memories with them. The same sort of dilemma follows her into the weekend. She knows she *should* go out on more dates with her husband but feels guilty that by doing so she is taking time away from the kids to be with their dad.

Both women in the chapter on resentment have highlighted negative aspects of a super commuter relationship and how resentment can creep into that relationship. Resentment is one of those emotions that gets stronger the longer you ignore it or let it simmer. Shedding light on it and being open with your partner can weaken its hold on you as a couple. If you don't address it, to paraphrase Sigmund Freud: What is repressed gets expressed.

If you are contemplating a super commuter relationship, are currently in one, or are just curious about the lives of those who are, I strongly encourage you to find ways to incorporate these three mottos into your daily life. Some people find it helpful to write them down and keep them near their computer, others hang them on their bathroom mirror, and some program them as an email alert that arrives at the same time each day. Another way to keep them present is to listen for them in the words of others. Can you find people in your life who already incorporate the three mottos? If so, use them as examples for your own life.

My ultimate goal in writing this book is to impart that there is no one right way to be a super commuter, but there most definitely are ways to make this non-traditional, but increasingly more common lifestyle less stressful for you and your family. In fact, you just heard from two-dozen people about how they do it and the common themes of their success stories. Some days will be hard and you will question why on earth you ever started a super commute. On other days you won't be able to imagine living any other way. For those readers who have no personal interest in super commuting, perhaps now you have gained some insight into why people who do super commute choose to live this way. It's quite possible you know some-one who super commutes—a neighbor, a co-worker, a relative—and maybe this book has sparked some ideas for ways you might be able to offer some assistance to them.

With that, I'd like to leave you with one last quote:

"Anything that's human is mentionable, and anything that is mentionable can be more manageable. When we can talk about our feelings, they become less overwhelming, less upsetting, and less scary. The people we trust with that important talk can help us know that we are not alone." —Fred Rogers

Epilogue

As the book comes to a close, many of you might be curious to hear my husband Ian's perspectives on super commuting. I therefore put to him the same questions I posed to my interviewees. Here are his reflections:

Why do you super commute?
"I received an amazing job offer in New York that advanced my career while providing financial security for my family. This latter consideration was especially important because prior to accepting this offer, Megan and I had suffered through some financially difficult times together. The events that transpired in the year and a half prior to me super commuting greatly impacted the decision to do it.

"In May of 2009 we were living in Los Angeles. We were upside down in our mortgage, our daughter had just turned two, and our son was only two months old. The company I had worked at for years was laying off people and my compensation had been cut nearly 37 percent. Our health insurance premium alone was $700 a month, as my company did not offer a family plan and like so many other Americans drowning in a sea of foreclosures and financial chaos, we were in tough shape. That August we happened to be in Minneapolis for Megan's brother's wedding. While there, I reached out to people I knew in the industry and lo and behold I landed a good job. Six weeks later I drove from Los Angeles to Minneapolis to start a new career in a new city while Megan and the kids packed up our house and she closed down her private practice.

"We felt so grateful to have been rescued from the abyss in California, but our euphoria proved to be short-lived. Since we had no place to live, we spent the first six months in Minneapolis sharing a townhouse with my sister-in-law. Megan, the two kids and I all slept in a 9x9 foot bedroom. It was a difficult winter, I worked all the time, our house in LA wasn't selling, and I was to discover that the company in Minneapolis was not doing well financially. It was intense and not a little scary. And then The Mill called. They are the best in the business at what they do and being asked to join the team was an honor. If the company in Minneapolis had been doing better, the decision might have been a bit more difficult one, but we were still struggling financially. We couldn't afford for me to be laid off and as it turns out, about a year after I left, the Minneapolis company did indeed go out of business."

What is your weekly departure and re-entry like?

"The commuting itself is hard but certainly manageable. People are adaptable over time and I think I'm highly adaptable in general. I usually take a 7:00 am flight Monday morning from Minneapolis and arrive at my desk in New York by noon. On Friday's, I head to the airport at 4:00 pm and if all goes as planned, I am home by 9:30 pm. It has been as late 1:00 am more than once due to weather or equipment problems. Is it frustrating having your flight delayed? Does waking up at 4:00 in the morning and working until 11:00 at night suck? Of course, but lots of people have it much worse. They have jobs they don't like or earn less then they need. Or both. When I land in Minneapolis on Friday evening I get in the car and sometimes I'll play music loud and sing at the top of my lungs. I find this helps me relax if it's been a hard week. If Megan is still awake, she greets me with a hug and a kiss. Our dog is usually very excited to see me and he likes me to chase him around for a bit. I go upstairs, kiss the kids, and go to bed. I always sleep better when Megan is next to me."

Did you make any sort of "after this is done . . ." plans?
"I thought I would do this for three years but now I don't know.
It's already been two and a half and I don't feel ready to stop. Our
kids are still young and they don't really remember when life was
different and it may seem weird to them to have me at home all the
time. We haven't really made any official plans for when I'm done
super commuting, but I have made some in my head. For example, I
would like to volunteer in my community or take classes at night."

What is the worst part of the super commute? What is the best?
"Megan and I would both agree that the financial security of
working at a successful company is the best part. I have also learned
so much at work. The experience and knowledge I gain every day is
career-defining. I work with smart, talented people and it's exciting
to be a part of that team.

"The worst part is that the super commute is very hard on
Megan. She has to juggle so much day in and day out, and even
though I try to do what I can on weekends, it's marginal compared
to what she deals with. She has had to rebuild her private practice
and be a single mom during the week to two young kids. It's a lot
and we are eternally grateful to her sister who lives with us and
helps out as much as her own work schedule and personal life allow.
She is like a second mom to the kids. When I worked in Minneapolis, the hours were long and I wasn't home much then either. When
I'm working in Minneapolis again, ideally it will be different but I
doubt those kinds of 8am-4pm jobs exist anymore. Our business
climate and culture have changed so dramatically in recent years."

**What do you and your partner do to stay connected emotionally
given the logistics of your lives?**
"We go on dates. We try and appreciate each other and the time we
have together. We have a weekend or two alone every year. During
the week our schedules make it hard to have any sort of set schedule

for connecting but Megan and the kids will often call from the car on speakerphone. I always like hearing their voices. It's the fuel that keeps me going. When I'm home we make sure we do some quality family stuff together."

Who turned out to be a bigger source of strength and support than you expected?

"Our neighbors are pretty helpful and very nice people. It is Megan's strength, however, that continues to amaze me. It is humbling to go home and see what she has to grapple with. Coming home every weekend reminds me of how essential my family is to me. With my wife and children beside me, I am everything. Without them I am nothing."

Did you feel like you could talk to people about any stress you were experiencing or that people could empathize?

"I have a few close friends who I can complain to. I have to exercise on a daily basis as much for my emotional as my physical health. When you super commute, you have to take care of yourself more than you normally would. I wasn't prepared for the learning curve of a new job combined with the pressures of traveling. Both are stressful and until you find your rhythm, it's hard."

If there were a support group for people in this situation, would you have attended?

"Since I learn by doing, if there were someone to follow through the process, a mentor for lack of a better word, that would have been most welcomed. The family stuff is going to be unique and specific to each couple. Before I started super commuting I spoke with a man who was already doing it and he made a very good point. He said it was much more about your spouse and his or her ability to deal with the commute. He was right. We super commuters have it easy. Those who remain behind and hold the fort are the ones who have it hard."

NOTES

Chapter 1

4. Rhymer Rigby, "Business Traveler: The Rise of the Super-Commuters," *The Financial Times,* December 27, 2011, http://www.ft.com/cms/s/0/2375423a-2c1d-11e1-b194-00144feabdc0.html#axzz2dHjJNw00.

4. Mitchell L. Moss and Carson Qing, "The Emergence of the 'Super-Commuter,'" Rudin Center for Transportation and Policy Management, New York University Wagner School of Public Service, February 2012, 2–4, 10, http://wagner.nyu.edu/rudincenter/publications.

5. "Number of full-time employees in the United States from 1990 to 2012 (in millions)," Statista, accessed August 22, 2013, http://www.statista.com/statistics/192356/number-of-full-time-employees-in-the-usa-since-1990.

5. Moss and Qing, "The Emergence of the 'Super-Commuter,'" 10–14.

6. Ted Gregory, "North Dakota's Oil Rush Lures Chicago-Area Residents," *Chicago Tribune,* March 17, 2013, http://articles.chicagotribune.com.

8. *The Cosby Show,* created by Bill Cosby, Michael Leeson, Ed. Weinberger (Encino, CA: Carsey-Werner Company, 1984–1992).

9. Pauline Boss, *Loss, Trauma, and Resilience: Therapeutic Work with Ambiguous Loss* (New York: W.W. Norton, 2006), 7–8.

9. Andrea Bernstein, "'Supercommuters' Board Airplanes to Get to Work," *Marketplace,* May 18, 2012, http://www.marketplace.org/topics/life/transportation-nation/supercommuters-board-airplanes-get-work.

10. Neil Demause, "Move. Certify. Repeat. State Requirements Create Career Hurdles for Relocating Military Spouses," *USAA Magazine,* Winter 2012,16–21.

Chapter 2

14. Susan Peae Gadoua, LCSW, "To Connect, Women Want to Talk and Men Want Sex—How Do Straight Couples Reconcile?" *Psychology Today,* February 7, 2010, http://www.psychologytoday.com/blog/contemplating-divorce/201002/connect-women-want-talk-and-men-want-sex-how-do-straight-couples-r.

16. "Telecommuting: Dream Come True?" PBS, November 14, 1997, http://www.pbs.org/newshour/forum/november97/telecommuting.html.

16. "About AOL: History," AOL, accessed March 28, 2013, http://corp.aol.com/category/overview.

17. *Up in the Air*. Directed by Jason Reitman. Starring George Clooney. (Hollywood, CA: Paramount Pictures, 2009).

18. Kahlil Gibran, *The Prophet* (New York: Alfred A. Knopf, 1968), 16.

18. Arthur G. Bedeian and Daniel A. Wren, "Most Influential Management Books of the 20th Century," *Organizational Dynamics* 29, no. 3 (Winter 2001): 221–225.

18. Douglas McGregor, *The Human Side of Enterprise* (New York: McGraw Hill,1960).

Chapter 3

22. Brett Paesel, *Mommies Who Drink* (New York: Grand Central Publishing, 2006).

23. Jad Mouawad, "Delta-Northwest Merger's Long and Complex Path," *The New York Times*, May 18, 2011, http://www.nytimes.com/2011/05/19/business/19air.html?pagewanted=all&_r=0.

26. William Shakespeare, "All's Well That Ends Well," *First Folio*, 1623.

27. "Crack," *The Free Dictionary*, accessed August 31, 2013. http://www.thefreedictionary.com/crack.

Chapter 4

36. Southern California super commuters: Moss and Qing, "The Emergence of the 'Super-Commuter,'" 10.

Chapter 5

39. Bruce Feiler, "Married but Sleeping Alone," *The New York Times*, July 25, 2010, http://www.nytimes.com/2010/07/25/fashion/25Family Matters.html?pagewanted=all&_r=0.

44. Elizabeth Weil, "Unmarried Spouses Have a Way With Words," *New York Times*, January 4, 2013, http://www.nytimes.com/2013/01/06/fashion/unmarried-spouses-have-a-way-with-words.html?pagewanted=all&_r=0.

44. "Statistics," Unmarried Equality, accessed April 19, 2013, http://Unmarried.org/statistics.

Chapter 6

52. Chris Mar, "Disney Dad," *Urban Dictionary*, September 23, 2012, accessed March 7, 2013, http://www.urbandictionary.com/define.php?term=disney+dad.

53. Mira Kirshenbaum, *When Good People Have Affairs: Inside the*

Hearts and Minds of People In Two Relationships (New York: St Martin's Griffin, 2008), 43–72.

Chapter 7

55. Tina Fey, *Bossypants* (New York: Reagan Arthur Books, 2011), 255.

58. Brett McKay and Kate McKay, "Making and Keeping Man Friendships," *The Art of Manliness* (blog), October 28, 2008, http://www.artofmanliness.com/2008/10/28/how-to-make-friends.

61. "What's 2e?" *Twice-Exceptional Newsletter*, accessed August 22, 2013, http://2enewsletter.com.

Chapter 8

65. Gibran, *The Prophet*, 15.

66. Average age: Moss and Qing, "The Emergence of the 'Super-Commuter,'" 6.

67. George James, "IN PERSON; A Survival Course for the Sandwich Generation," *The New York Times,* January 17, 1999, http://www.nytimes.com/1999/01/17/nyregion/in-person-a-survival-course-for-the-sandwich-generation.html?pagewanted=all&src=pm.

67. Carol Abaya: Sandwichgeneration.com.

68. Corridor principle: Heidi Neck, "It Takes Kinetic Energy to Turn an Idea Into a Business," *Forbes*, June 13, 2102, http://www.forbes.com/ sites/ babson/2012/06/13it-takes-kinetic-energy-to-turn-an-idea-into- a-business.

71. William Forrester, "What Part of the Middle East is a Great Gay Destination?" *Advocate*, September 5, 2102, http://www.advocate.com/travel/destinations/2012/09/05/what-part-middle-east-great-gay-destination?page=full.

Chapter 9

76. "ADAPT: After Deployment: Adaptive Parenting Tools," University of Minnesota, Department of Family Social Science, accessed March 11, 2013, http://www.cehd.umn.edu/fsos/projects/adapt/default.asp.

81. "Requirements SCQL—Unit Production Manager," DGACA, accessed August 22, 2013, http://www.dgaca.org/sc-specific-requirements/sc-upm.

81. "Requirements NYQL—Unit Production Manager," DGACA-East, accessed August, 22, 2013, http://www.dgaca-east.org/specific-requirements/upm-specific-requirements.

81. Diana Lodderhose, "Runaways Welcome: Countries Offer Incentives To Lure Productions Fleeing Hollywood," *Variety*, August 29, 2013, http://variety.com/2013/biz/news/runaways-welcome-countries-offer-incentives-to-lure-productions-fleeing-hollywood-1200590312.

82. Randee Dawn, "Hollywood In a State of Emergency Over 'Runaway Production,'" *Today,* accessed August 27, 2013, http://www.today.com entertainment/hollywood-state-emergency-over-runaway-production-8C11009958.

82. Richard Verrier, "Los Angeles Losing the Core of Its TV Production to Other States," *Los Angeles Times*, August, 15, 2012, http://articles.latimes.com/2012/aug/15/business/la-fi-ct-runaway-tv-20120814.

82. Chicago Film Tour, accessed March 20, 2013, http://www.chicago-filmtour.com.

82. "Dawson's Creek Tour," Hook, Line, and Paddle, accessed March 20, 2013, http://www.hooklineandpaddle.com/tripsinstruction/dawsons-creek-tour.

84. "The DGA-Producer Health Plan," Directors Guild of America-Producer, accessed August 23, 2013, http://www.dgaplans.org/health.htm.

85. "MOMS Clubs," Moms Offering Moms Support, accessed August 23, 2013, https://www.momsclub.org.

Chapter 11

93. Otsuichi, *Zoo* (San Francisco: Viz Media, LLC, 2009).

93. Six guidelines: Boss, *Loss, Trauma, and Resilience*, 71.

94. Reconstructing Identity: Boss, *Loss, Trauma, and Resilience*, 124.

95. Tempering Mastery: Boss, *Loss, Trauma, and Resilience*, 99, 104.

95. "Mastery," *The Free Dictionary*, accessed August 30, 2013, http://www.thefreedictionary.com/mastery.

95. Kaleel Jamison,*The Nibble Theory and the Kernel of Power: A Book About Leadership, Self-Empowerment, and Personal Growth* (Ramsey, NJ: Paulist Press, 1984), 63.

95. Overwhelm: Boss, *Loss, Trauma, and Resilience*, 111.

95. Groups: Boss, *Loss, Trauma, and Resilience*, 106.

96. Finding Meaning: Boss, *Loss, Trauma, and Resilience*, 94-95.

96. Normalizing Ambivalence: Boss, *Loss, Trauma, and Resilience*, 144.

96. Presence of ambivalence: Boss, *Loss, Trauma, and Resilience*, 145.

96. Coping: Boss, *Loss, Trauma, and Resilience*, 158 .

96. Revising Attachment: Boss, *Loss, Trauma, and Resilience*, 176.

97. Discovering Hope: Boss, *Loss, Trauma, and Resilience*, 182.

98. Lao-Tzu, *Tao Te Ching*, Trans. Stephen Mitchell (NewYork: Harper Perennial, 2006) 67.

Chapter 12

99. Susan Piver, *The Hard Questions: 100 Questions to Ask Before You Say "I Do,"* (New York: Tarcher/Putnam, 2000).

100. Piver, *Hard Questions*, 52.

101. Chellie Campbell, *Zero to Zillionaire*, (Sourcebooks, 2006), 59–60.

103. Blank Slate Concept: Nancy McWilliams, *Psychoanalytic Psychotherapy: A Practitioner's Guide* (New York: The Guilford Press, 2004), 15.

104. Miracle Question: John L. Walter and Jane E. Peller, *Becoming Solution-Focused In Brief Therapy* (Levittown, PA: Brunner/Mazel, 1992), 73.

106. "The 'Original' Daddy Dolls and Hug a Hero Dolls," Daddy Dolls, Inc., accessed April 9, 2013, https://www.daddydolls.com/store/hugahero-dolls.

107. Anonymous, *Record a Story: Sesame Street Together at Heart*, (Lincolnwood, IL: Publications International Ltd, 2010).

109. "Commuting and Traveling," The Port Authority of New York City and New Jersey, accessed August 27, 2013, http://www.panynj.gov/commuting-traveling.html.

110. "NYC Airports to Manhattan Transportation FAQ," Flyerguide, accessed August 27, 2013, http://www.flyerguide.com/wiki/index.php/NYC_Airports_to_Manhattan_Transportation_FAQ.

110. "How To Apply," Global Entry, accessed May 2, 2013, http://www.globalentry.gov/howtoapply.html.

111. "AirTrain JFK," *MTA*, accessed August 27, 2013, http://web.mta.info/mta/airtrain.htm.

112. "Snap Shot Postcard," http://www.snapshotpostcard.com/solution.

113. Wunderlist.com.

114. "What Is Skype?" Skype, http://www.skype.com/en/what-is-skype.

114. Viber, accessed September 25, 2013, http://www.viber.com/faq.

114. "Staycation," *Merriam-Webster*, accessed August 27, 2013, http://www.merriam-webster.com/dictionary/staycation.

115. "Florida Resident Cruise Discounts," *Cruise Cheap*, accessed August 31, 2013, http://www.cruisecheap.com/cruises/florida-residents.html.

115. Therapist search: Psychologytoday.com.

116. "What Services Does an EAP Offer?" *Department of Labor*,

accessed August 27, 2013, http://www.dol.gov/elaws/asp/drugfree/drugs/assistance/Screen94.asp.

Chapter 13

119. La Leche League International, accessed August 31, 2013, http://www.llli.org.

119. Mommy and Me, accessed August 31, 2013, http://www.mommyandme.com.

119. Johannes Nielsen, "Single Parents in the Nordic Countries," *Nordic Social-Statistical Committee*, (2004) 35.

120. Marcy Axness, PhD, *Parenting For Peace: Raising the Next Generation of Peacemakers* (Boulder, CO: Sentient Publications, 2012).

125. ChrisMar, "Disney Dad."

127. "Secrets to a Happy Marriage: Get a Little Bit Divorced," *Good Housekeeping*, accessed April 15, 2013, http://www.goodhousekeeping.com/family/marriage-sex/happy-marriage-tips.

Chapter 14

131. Janet Bristow and Victoria Galo, "The Significance of Three," *The Shawl Ministry*, 1998, http://www.shawlministry.com/significance_of_three.htm.

132. "Motto," *Merriam-Webster*. accessed September 18, 2013. http://www.merriam-webster.com/dictionary/motto.

133. Women Leaving Medicine, http://www.womenleavingmedicine.com.

138. Sigmund Freud, *The Basic Writings of Sigmund Freud (Psychopathology of Everyday Life, the Interpretation of Dreams, and Three Contributions to the Theory of Sex)*, trans. A.A. Brill (New York: Modern Library, 1995), 140.

Epilogue

142. The Mill and Mill+, http://www.themill.com.

Appendix

Questions and Exercises

Sometimes the questions are complicated
and the answers are simple.
—Dr. Seuss

The Super Commute

1. Name one benefit from super commuting that you might not have in a "regular" job. Or in other words, what might this lifestyle allow you to do that otherwise you might not be able to do?

2. Is there a part of your relationship that is not "traditional"?
   Are you okay with that?
   Are there people in your life who are not?

3. How do you prefer to communicate? Phone? Texting? Email? Face to face?

4. While apart, what events will each of you likely call your spouse about?

5. Have you created a check-in phrase to determine each other's frame of mind before launching into your day, whether it be good or bad? Such a phrase can be as simple as "Are you up for talking?" or answering the phone with "I've had a hard day so I'm not really in the mood to talk much."

6. When is the last time you thanked your partner for something? It doesn't have to be for something big. It could be for something as simple as emptying the dishwasher.

Children

1. Can you and your children establish routines or traditions that provide connection with the parent who is away? What might some of those routines be?

2. How might your children answer the miracle question? (If you woke up tomorrow and everything was the way you wanted it to be, what would life be like?)

3. Does your local fitness club offer low-cost childcare as part of the monthly membership?

4. Is there a local college that might have students interested in babysitting?

5. How many activities are your children involved in? Do they truly enjoy them or does the stress of those commitments overshadow the value?

6. If you were to drop one activity, what would you do with that time?

Self-Care

1. What kind of self-care is helpful for you?
   Do you do it regularly or does it take a crisis or illness before you make time for it?

2. Can you find the silver lining in a difficult situation?

3. When is the last time you completed a household budget?

4. Where in your budget can you make small savings to free up money to make your life a little easier? For example, to hire a person to do a thorough cleaning of the house once a month or a lawn service for mowing.

5. If you could afford to hire help, how would you spend that extra time?

6. What is a dream that you have yet to pursue or a hobby that you have put aside?
   What is holding you back?
   Does your partner have one?

7. Can each of you support the other in adding this element to your life?

8. Name one commitment you have that you wish you didn't have.
   Can you stop doing it?
   Can you transform it into something more fulfilling?

9. What is the one chore or responsibility that causes you the most stress?

10. If your partner agreed to take over that chore or responsibility, could you let him or her do it as he or she wished to do it or does it have to be done your way?

The Should's

On a scale of 1–10, how are you feeling right now? 1 means overwhelmed, stressed out, you can't think straight, and 10 means your life is great and you are totally carefree. Now draw a line down the middle of a piece of paper and list to the left of the line as many things that come to mind when you say this sentence:

"I should" . . . For example, "I should" send out holiday cards. "I should" lose ten pounds, or "I should" serve on a committee at work.

Now take a moment and ask yourself, after writing those words, how are you feeling on that same scale from 1 to 10? More stressed? Overwhelmed? Excited? Crabby?

Next, across from each "should" you listed, write down who says you should? Is it you, your job, society, your family?

Finally, go through the list and re-read each line as, "I would like to" instead of "I should" and cross off the ones that don't resonate with you as something you truly would like to do. For the ones you didn't cross out, think about why you aren't doing them. If you crossed them all off, what *would* you like to be doing?

What is the first step you need to take to start doing the thing you *would* like to do?

Who in your life can help you take that first step?

RECOMMENDED READING AND WEBSITES

Books

Girls Will Be Girls: Raising Confident and Courageous Daughters by JoAnn Deak, PhD, with Teresa Barker

What to Do When You Worry Too Much: A Kids Guide to Overcoming Anxiety by Dawn Huebner, PhD

Perfectionism: What's Bad about Being Too Good? by Miriam Adderholdt, PhD & Jan Goldberg

Eating in the Light of the Moon: How Women Can Let Go of Compulsive Eating Through Metaphor and Storytelling by Anita Johnston, PhD

Trees Make the Best Mobiles: Simple Ways to Raise Your Child in a Complex World by Jessica Teich and Brandel France de Bravo

Record a Story: Sesame Street, Together at Heart, Publications International Ltd

Parenting for Peace: Raising the Next Generation of Peacemakers by Marcy Axness, PhD

Where to Draw the Line by Anne Katherine, MA

The Hard Questions: 100 Questions to Ask Before You Say "I Do" by Susan Piver

When Good People Have Affairs: Inside the Hearts and Minds of People in Two Relationships by Mira Kirshenbaum

What is Narrative Therapy? An Easy-to-Read Introduction by Alice Morgan

Quiet: The Power of Introverts In a World That Can't Stop Talking by Susan Cain

Off-Ramps and On-Ramps: Keeping Talented Women on the Road to Success by Sylvia Ann Hewlett

Daring Greatly: How the Courage to Be Vulnerable Transforms the Way We Live, Love, Parent, and Lead by Brené Brown, PhD, LMSW

Websites

www.supercommutercouples.com

www.yapta.com

www.flyerguide.com

www.dosomething.org

www.momsclub.org

www.tripit.com

www.wunderlist.com

www.volunteermatch.org

Acknowledgments

A huge thank you to:

All of the super commuter couples who so openly shared their stories with me. I learned so much and am honored to be able to pass along your wisdom and experiences to others.

My editor Bill Hammond. Your honesty, patience, knowledge, and deep pool of experience were invaluable in this process.

Dorie McClelland at Spring Book Design. A true artist.

Pat Morris of Book Architects: Thank you for your feedback, guidance, and eye for all that is grammatically correct.

My Minneapolis and Los Angeles colleagues and especially my former supervisors Arlene Butler, Lyra Barrera, Marianne Diaz, & Giselle Terry. I am so grateful for all that I have learned, and still learn, from you.

Mitchell Moss and Carson Qing at NYU's Rudin Center for Transportation & Policy Management: Your cutting-edge research on the rise of super commuting has shined a light on this growing trend in our global society.

Dr. Pauline Boss: Your pioneering work in the field of trauma and ambiguous loss is a gift to the field of psychology.

Bill O'Brien and Terry Davis (My two favorite literature and composition teachers): You pushed your students to be better writers and fostered a love of reading in us. I worked as a CPA and now am a therapist, but I have never forgotten your classes, and I am excited to add author to that list of achievements. You were integral in that. Thank you.

Stephanie Ross: You've helped out in multiple ways: your feedback, your recommendations, your enthusiasm for the project, and the motivating coffee meet-ups.

Dean Carpentier: In a matter of minutes you took my nebulous idea and turned it into an amazing cover. Your photography and design talents are impressive, not to mention your writing. We will see *Drag* on the screen one day!

Paula Himel: A cheerleader from day one. Thank you for keeping me motivated, brainstorming with me, and for my much-needed Boulder weekend once the manuscript was finished.

Carrie and Kevin Renville; Barb Nickel and Gregg Defoe: Thank you for your years of friendship and extra thanks to Kevin for arranging the hotel room so I could sequester myself and finalize the book.

Pat, Connie, Reina, Liz, Aretha, Chris, Danielle, Michelle, and New Horizon Academy-Maple Grove: Thank you for taking such great care of our kids over the past 6 years. You are truly part of our village.

Jacki, Sue, Charlie, Suzie, Chuckie and the rest of the extended Bearce, Elliot, and Scott families. Thank you for your encouragement, love, and support. I couldn't have asked for a better family to marry into.

My sister Kelly Sinkbeil: There is no way I could do this without you. From your emotional and practical support to your love for the kids, and of course your mad cleaning skills, it all helps control the chaos and keep me sane.

My super creative brother Mark Sinkbeil: Your talents amaze me. From the beginning you've helped create my brand, my website, the book cover, and answer all my tech questions and make it seem effortless. And of course, all the fun times with uncle Mark and aunt Lana.

My parents Jim and Merry: We owe you so much. Helping with the kids, moving us, moving us again, never-ending house projects, the daily phone calls, your unconditional love and encouragement. I could go on and on. Thank you! Thank you! Thank you!

Katherine and Austin: I love you very much! Thank you for being you.

Ian: My best friend and partner on this crazy journey called life. Who could've predicted the last few years? Thank you for suggesting I tell the world about it. I'm very proud of you and thank you for working so hard. Here's to another 60 years! I love you!

Megan Bearce, MA, LMFT,
is a licensed marriage and family therapist
who specializes in providing support to super
commuter couples. She holds a bachelor of
science in accounting from Minnesota State
University, Mankato, and a master of arts in
clinical psychology from Antioch University

Los Angeles. In addition to her private practice, she writes and
speaks about topics such as perfectionism, parenting gifted girls,
and women's issues in the workforce. She is currently developing a
training program to educate therapists about working with super
commuter clients. Megan lives in Minneapolis, Minnesota, with her
super commuter husband and their two children.